To Bob
Love
Lyn

a view
from
the
steeple

Other Books by the Author

Pennies From a Poor Box
Straws From the Crib
Sanctity on the Sidewalk

● ● ●

[The following were published by Our Sunday Visitor]
Happiness Over the Hill
Stay With Us, Lord
Give God Equal Time
Stumbling Toward Heaven
Ten Responsible Minutes

FATHER MANTON

a view from the steeple

Our Sunday Visitor, Inc.
Huntington, Indiana 46750

Imprimi Potest:
Rev. Edward J. Gilbert, C.SS.R.
Provincial

Our Sunday Visitor, Inc.
200 Noll Plaza
Huntington, Indiana 46750

INTERNATIONAL STANDARD BOOK NUMBER
0-87973-591-0

LIBRARY OF CONGRESS CATALOG CARD NUMBER
85-60519

Cover design by James E. McIlrath

PRINTED IN THE UNITED STATES OF AMERICA

591

c o n t e n t s

CHAPTER 5: HUMAN QUIRKS

CHAPTER 6: INSIDE THE CHURCH

CHAPTER 7: SILHOUETTE OF THE SAVIOR

CHAPTER 8: FIRST LADY

CHAPTER 9: BASKET OF FRAGMENTS

chapter one

PORTRAIT GALLERY

{ Cardinal Wright Remembered }

Though it may sound like something snipped out of a second nocturn in the old Breviary, it is a fact that John Wright was developing a devotion to our Blessed Mother even back in his boyhood days. Every Wednesday afternoon he hiked up the hill from Boston Latin School to the tall twin spires and booming bells of Mission Church, trooping along with the throng gathered for the novena in honor of Our Mother of Perpetual Help.

The years rolled on, Mission Church became a basilica, and the young student became John Cardinal Wright. In 1974 (if I may intrude the personal) he did me the great honor of preaching there at my golden jubilee as a Redemptorist. By that time arthritis had begun its crippling work on his overburdened legs, so I gently hinted that he deliver his homily from the lectern on the floor of the sanctuary instead of climbing the high marble pulpit. His response was almost a glare: "I'll preach from that pulpit if it is the last thing I do!" And he did, with the usual masterly flow of phrase and the trembling fire which were his trademark.

On that occasion he shook his head sadly over how much the neighborhood around the church had changed. Thereafter, whenever he wrote me here, he would always scrawl at the bottom of the stately formal Vatican envelope in his own bold black handwriting: OPPOSITE FUNERAL PARLOR.

In part this was an allusion to the fact that I have lived in the same room with the same somber view for some forty-five years. I never told him that the boarded-up drugstore next to the funeral parlor had been the scene of a double murder, and that in the pie-shop next to that the baker had gotten a bullet in the belly. No wonder the crowds stopped coming to the basilica!

But the neighborhood around Boston's majestic cathedral in another part of town has changed too, and that reminds me of a day when Father Wright stole the show in the cathedral without opening his mouth. The occasion was the funeral Mass of Cardinal O'Connell, who could give the Boston Brahmins lessons in lofty manners. When the cardinal died, Father Wright was his secretary. At the lordly obsequies, down the long cathedral aisle marched a sizable part of the national hierarchy: monsignori, bishops, archbishops, cardinals — a gorgeous pageant of flowing purples and scarlets and crimsons. And in the midst of it, almost like a fly on a stained-glass window, was one priest in a simple black cassock with a light black Roman cape billowing behind him. In his outstretched hands Father Wright carried the letter of condolence from the pope. Everybody was wondering who was that sole bit of black in the huge Red Sea.

Somehow that incident brings to mind another event. That was Boston's biggest demonstration in honor of the Holy Name, a spectacle like the American Legion parade, that tramped on for hours upon hours. The formal attire of a bishop in those undemocratic days was silk hat and morning coat, and the recently "ordained" Bishop Wright swung along in the front rank, waving an arm of recognition right and left, flashing his eyes like a young Italian prince, a genuine specimen of the "dark Irish."

In those days, his personal architecture was slimly Gothic, before the inexorable years turned it into rotund Romanesque. Far from a towering presence, he favored the squat French miter rather than the monumental beehive headdress preferred by many bishops. This may have been influenced by his first years in the priesthood when he spent his university vacations as a curate in a tiny French village. Or was he a Francophile because of his long-standing interest in Saint Joan of Arc? Certainly he had amassed the most complete collection of Arcania in this country, an incredible array of volumes now lining the shelves of the Bishop Cheverus Room in the Boston Public Library. (Bishop Cheverus, incidentally, was Boston's first Catholic bishop, and if anyone doubts that he was French, let me list the litany of his names: Jean Louis Anne Madeleine Lefebvre de Cheverus. May one doubt that the Indians for whom he worked in the Maine woods ever called him all that?)

John Wright was a much simpler handle, and in so many ways he was a simple man: simple in the sense of un-affected. As a cardinal — resident in Rome and the head of a Vatican Congregation (the man in charge of all the Catholic clergy throughout the world) — he wore the crimson robes of his office when ceremony or protocol demanded it; but otherwise he confined himself to unpretentious black. I recall him in a plain black cassock guiding me in my American black suit through the streets of Rome to a restaurant. "No tourist trap, here!" he boasted. "No American has been in this place for twenty years." Then he and the waiter put on a pleasant act, arguing up and down the menu about just what to order. It was all like a scene from an opera, and it made me remember that the cardinal had captained his debating team at Boston Latin and Boston College.

Debater he was; athlete, never. Call him the ultimate

intellectual for whom sports simply did not exist. Like the old priest in the film *Going My Way*, he would "not know which end of a caddy to hold." He used to say with a wry smile that if ever he should get the notion to exercise, he would banish it like a bad thought. This is a pity because more activity would have meant less weight, and weight, I suspect, was one of the grim factors that did him in at the end.

Some priests play tennis; some play golf. Some fish and some ski. As priest, bishop, and cardinal, John Wright hardly walked. You could not even say about him (as you can about many) that he walked only as far as his car, because he did not even drive. The car picked him up. What he did do was run up and down columns of print, and it was an exception if his bed lamp clicked off before two in the morning. The day was for working and the night was for reading — or better, for studying, because his literary fare was never frothy snow-pudding but solid and even heavy stuff, with theology and history as the main courses.

Into this deep well of knowledge he dropped the bucket of an insatiably curious mind and brought up the material for his lectures and sermons. All his life he had far more invitations to speak than he could ever honor. Yet, for a tremendously popular preacher he did not have the deep, rich voice that rolls out glorious tones like a cathedral organ. On the contrary his timbre tended to be thin and pitched a bit high, but one forgot all that in his dynamic projection. Far from a monotonous, level, railroad-track delivery, he had the curves and dips, the unexpected rises and swoops of a roller coaster. By lingering on a word, he could drop over it an interpretation like an ermine cape that gave it an importance it normally never had. He would hit an emphatic phrase with the crispness of a hammer. His was the unconscious art of the born actor, blended with the conviction of the dedicated apostle. It all came out as the art of the really rare orator who taught you, persuaded you, moved you.

Incidentally, one of his chief weapons was wit. Light-hearted humor laced his serious messages like playful whitecaps on a deep sea. He loved to laugh.

Beneath all this, of course, lay the strong, solid foundation of the spiritual. Without it, the rest (in him or in any of us) is mere crepe paper. *"Resonare Christum!"* he chose as the motto for his coat of arms: "To re-echo Christ!" A completely involved churchman with no outside interests whatever, he lived entirely for God and for the spread of God's kingdom. Even the Vatican has to have its bureaucracy, and Cardinal Wright administered one of those bureaus (the clergy), but he never let the desk loom so large that it blotted out the prie-dieu or the altar. God, not government (even ecclesiastical), always came first. Many a time he came away from a high-level think-tank at the Vatican to set out for a period of prayer at some shrine of our Lady. A graybeard in wisdom, he was childlike in his simple, unassuming piety.

On Sunday afternoons he loved to take a ride through the Roman countryside, eventually reaching some spot dedicated to the Madonna. More often than not, his ride took him along the Appian Way to the shrine of Our Lady of Divine Love. Another favorite destination, in the town of Genezzano, was the chapel with the famous painting of Our Lady of Good Counsel. If the cardinal had brought along some priest for the ride, he would first point to the plaque next to the picture that said, "Pope Pius IX made a pilgrimage to this Marian shrine prior to the opening of Vatican Council I." Then the cardinal would stride to the opposite wall and read aloud the other plaque: "Pope John XXIII visited this shrine prior to the opening of Vatican Council II." Finally the cardinal would whirl around and say with darting eyes, "I wonder how many of those who speak equivocally about the spirit of Vatican II are aware that it started here?"

As a newly ordained priest (Mary was never far from his priesthood), he had said his second Mass at the Roman shrine of the Madonna della Strada; but his very first Mass was touching enough to be in honor of Mary, Comforter of the Afflicted. In a letter to his parents written that week he says:

> No one pays much attention to blind kids, and their asylum here is a bleak enough place — so I thought I'd find it inspiring for me, and perhaps a little pleasure for them, if I celebrated my first Mass among them and for them.
>
> I at least received *my part* of that hope! The Mass was at 6:30 A.M., with a choir of blind boys singing and a blind boy at the organ. The children (sixty boys and thirty girls) received Holy Communion, and as long as I live I shall have in my eyes the sight of those blind kids kneeling at the altar.
>
> It was too grand to be saddening. No thrill you can imagine could equal mine when I had the privilege of placing the Host on the tongues of those splendid sons and daughters of God, while asking Christ to keep them close to Him and bring them to life everlasting.
>
> After Mass I sat on a great chair before the high altar and each boy and girl was led forward for my first blessing. Many of them would smile and say, "Thank you" — so grateful for the tiniest recognition are these youngsters.

This somehow resurrects the memory of something Cardinal Wright said about the Boy Jesus. You have to realize that perhaps because the cardinal had once taught theology, he had small patience with pretentious new theories that were as far out from the old doctrine as satellites are from Earth. He felt an almost personal grief that, as he phrased it, "the clear fixed stars of the Catholic faith are momentarily obscured by theological smog." Someone once asked him what he thought of the recent theory that it dawned on Christ only gradually that He was the Son of God. Cardinal Wright answered with withering sarcasm: "I can see it all so plainly. The twelve-year-old Boy bursts into the kitchen at Nazareth; He runs up to His Mother and blurts out, 'Gee, Mom, guess WHAT!' "

As his favorite Marian shrine was Lourdes, his favorite Marian devotion was the rosary. He was wont to wrinkle a disapproving nose at the mention of a wake service that featured a few verses of Scripture and a couple of sentimental poems. He liked to point out that the greater part of the rosary was scooped right out of the Scriptures, and that most funeral-parlor poetry was pious fluff. "When I am laid out," he would say, "start the beads. And if no one has a pair, look in my pocket. They will be there, unless the undertaker has taken them out."

I wonder how many times he was part of the candle-lit rosary processions at Lourdes? Once he invited me to be his guest on the White Train. At that time all I knew was that the White Train was in some manner connected with Lourdes. I learned the hard way and loved it. It was called the White Train because of the white banners slung along the sides, but more so because of the white uniforms of the dozens of doctors and nurses aboard. It was an annual trip that carried about three hundred and fifty sick priests who were brought from all over Italy to the railway yard in Rome for a pilgrimage to Lourdes.

Blind priests, crippled priests, priests with cancer and other kinds of diseases — all filled the long train. We did not remove our clothes to rest or sleep during the whole thirty-hour trip, but who could complain when you saw such helplessness all around you? At each of the half-dozen stations where we stopped, the priests and people of the town were there with food. (We had set out with nothing.) While the pasta and fruit and salami and the rest were taken aboard, Cardinal Wright was on the platform, bullhorn in hand, addressing the crowd. As he spoke, they laughed, they applauded, they blinked back tears, they were in the palm of his hand. Admiration and affection sparkled in their eyes. By the last stop, though, he was hoarse and limp.

Around the parklike grounds of Lourdes you would come upon the cardinal pushing a wheelchair or pulling a rolling stretcher bed. On the last morning, he was the chief celebrant at the farewell Mass. As at the Last Supper, there were twelve bishops around the altar. As on Pentecost, the readings (very brief) were in five different languages. And, like the sick who came to Christ in Galilee, there were three hundred and fifty sick priests in rows upon rows of wheelchairs, bright stoles over their bathrobes, concelebrating. As many more of us who were healthy (perhaps three hundred more) said our part of the Mass from the pews. Cardinal Wright never seemed more the head of the clergy of the world than in that sacred hour.

Now, in a final sense, his own pilgrimage as a sick priest is over and he has reached home. At last he is with the Lady he loved and the Lord he served.

But, for many of us, his memory lingers on.

{ Pius X }

During his eleven years as pope, Pius X canonized only four saints. One of them, if we may interject a local commercial, was the Redemptorist priest Saint Clement Hofbauer. Pius X himself was the first pope to be canonized since Saint Pius V, three hundred years before. There were, of course, many holy men on the Chair of Peter in those three centuries; but there is a towering difference between saintly and saint . . . at least in the official, technical sense. A museum may have on its walls many superb pictures, but a work by Leonardo da Vinci or Raphael is rare.

Joseph Cardinal Sarto never expected to be pope. It must have been a picturesque procession that balmy May morning in Venice when a little fleet of gondolas pointed their prows like proud swans down the Grand Canal, past the handsome palaces of various colors: some light blue, some pale pink, some buff, with flowers glowing in the window boxes and, here and there, strands of seaweed stirring on the steps like a soaked morning newspaper.

When the gondolas came to the railway station, the cardinal took his place on the rear platform of the train, looking like a Florentine portrait with his silver hair, sculptured face, and flaming robe. He said a brief good-bye and asked those present to pray that the Holy Spirit would guide the consistory in picking the right man for the papacy. Then he blessed them and was about to move inside when someone in the crowd called out, "Eminenza, don't forget to come back to us!" He turned and, smiling, reached into his robe and waved his railway ticket, saying, "Of course I'll be back. See? I have my return ticket!"

But Cardinal Sarto did not come back. In those days, when the new pope was announced to the cardinals in the Sistine Chapel, the canopy over each cardinal's throne would fall, except that of the cardinal chosen to be pope. This was the sign for the other cardinals to come forward and pledge their loyalty to the successor of Saint Peter. So by the vote of the sacred college, Cardinal Sarto of Venice became Pope Pius X.

A few hours later the eldest of the cardinals, the dean, slipped into the chapel to say a prayer. There he saw the new pontiff in his new white robe, praying, with tears on his cheeks. The old cardinal touched him softly on the shoulder, saying, "Don't worry, Your Holiness. The God who gave you the wisdom to guide the gondola of Saint Mark, the little church of Venice, will also give you the greater wisdom to guide the ship of Peter, the universal Church."

Pius X was not a scholar like his predecessor, Leo XIII, whose letters to the world pleading for a just wage for the workingman sounded the first shot heard round the world for labor unions. Pius X was not a diplomat like his successor, Pius XI, who negotiated the concordat with the Italian government that established Vatican State. Pius X was primarily a priest, a parish priest in a white cassock whose parish was the world. But he was essentially the bishop of Rome, so that got him special attention.

Every Sunday afternoon in a section of the Vatican gardens (or, in inclement weather, indoors) Pope Pius X would preach to a different parish, each taking its turn. A simple man (not a stupid one: you do not become head of the Church if your brain is only a forty-watt bulb), he spoke on simple, straightforward themes like the Ten Commandments, the seven sacraments, the truths of the Apostles' Creed, and the mysteries of the rosary (which really are not mysteries but the events in the life of our Lord and our Lady).

Speaking of the rosary, Pius X had a warm childlike love for our Lady. When he built a new seminary to educate the priests of Rome, he ordered that each seminarian's room should be monastically simple. On the walls should hang only two things, a crucifix and a picture of the Madonna. Which Madonna? Pius X chose the one he loved best: the picture of Our Mother of Perpetual Help.

Just as it takes a doctor to evaluate the knowledge and skill of doctors, and a lawyer to appreciate the ability of lawyers, the clergy more than the laity can appreciate the contributions to the Church of Pius X. Take, for example, canon law, which was recently revised to harmonize with Vatican II. Up to the time of Pius X the laws of the Church were scattered through so many volumes that only a professional knew even where to look for them. Pius X saw to it that the important laws were streamlined, grouped under the right headings, and gathered into one single volume.

In the same way, the Breviary — from which the priest reads as his daily prayers — was hopelessly involved and prolonged (it took about an hour and a half each day). Pius X rearranged this to make it shorter and more compact, and yet every day the priest reads a brief biography or commentary on that day's saint and still covers the one hundred and fifty psalms each week.

Possibly because he came from a peasant village, Pius X was a down-to-earth, straight-to-the-point, completely no-nonsense man. At one meeting of the cardinals in the Curia — when they were bewailing the melancholy state of the world, and suggesting grand programs — Pius X ended the meeting by getting up and smiling and saying, "Gentlemen, I have an infallible plan to reform the world. Let each of us begin with himself."

When the case called for it, Pius X could be stern as granite. To us who look back down the long corridors of the past eighty years, it is ironic that the movement was called Modernism — though now it has only the stale and moldy smell of something long dead. Those "Catholic" theologians set out to dilute the supernatural, to chip away at the divinity of Christ, to whittle down the crucifix. They wondered about the Virgin Birth. They speculated about the Resurrection. They conjectured about the Real Presence of our Lord in the Blessed Sacrament. It was compromise on every front. To the straightforward Pius X they were only like rats nibbling or gnawing at sacred truths and basic doctrines.

Possibly they thought that he was only a naïve, simple man who did not see the implications of their teaching. But all at once the kindly, humble pope became the Christ swinging the knotted cord and driving these doctrine changers out of the temple, overturning their tables piled with false teachings.

But on another front Pius was the gentle, welcoming Christ who had said, "Let the little children come unto Me!" Up to now the usual age at which children received their first communion was fourteen. Pius X changed it to when the child reached the use of reason, usually around the age of seven. But he was not only the apostle of early communion for children but also of frequent communion for adults. Before that time even good Catholics received at Easter only (to fulfill their Easter duty), and perhaps at Christmas in the glow of the feast — possibly also at a family anniversary or the like. Christ was in the Tabernacle, the people were in the pews, and the communion rail rose like a polished marble fence between them.

That empty communion rail was the fruit of a heresy called Jansenism. The Jansenists claimed that people were not worthy to receive communion frequently. To which Pius X rejoined that no one was worthy to receive communion any time! He said none of us receives Christ because he is worthy but to become better. There are, he pointed out, different roads to heaven. There is innocence, but that is for children. There is penance, but we shy away from that. There is the acceptance of trials that heaven sends us, but we ask to be freed from them. For adults the surest way to heaven is frequent, fervent communion.

When Pius X died in 1914, his will revealed that he did not want to be embalmed and that he be buried not among the impressive tombs in Saint Peter's but in the basement, the crypt. So he was, but people made their way down there day after day. They left flowers — not grand floral pieces but little homegrown bouquets. They brought flowers and they prayed, and soon tales went around about miraculous cures. This grew so much that there had to be an official investigation in skeptical Rome. As a result, certain undoubted healings wrought through his intercession were certified as miraculous. So it came about that this man who had never aspired to bishop's purple, never coveted the cardinal's red hat, never dreamed of wearing papal white, was declared in 1954 in a gloriously illuminated Saint Peter's — with Sistine Choir singing and silver trumpets blaring — a canonized saint.

There is a further happy footnote to this story. While the new saint's tomb was being prepared in the main body of Saint Peter's, Pope John XXIII ordered that the body in its handsome new casket should be taken to the cathedral of Saint Mark in Venice. There it lay in solemn state for three days.

So Pius X *did* keep his word. He *did* come back, after all.

{ Pius XI }

The curtain rises on the life of Achille Ratti, with the majestic Alps for a backdrop. His village was Desio, called that by the Roman legions because it meant a tramp of ten (or *decem*) miles from Milan. On a clear day the glistening Alpine peaks seemed to tower up right at the end of the main street. Always they wore the snowy robe of a pope; always they were crowned with a tiara of jeweled ice. Someday, he promised himself, he would get up there to the very top. He meant the peak, did not dream of the papacy.

In 1890 he stood, alpenstock in hand, on the summit of Mount Blanc, the first Italian to conquer that formidable mountain. In 1922 he stood on the summit of

Christendom, in his hand the crosier of the Chief Shepherd and about him the white cassock of the pope. An Alpinist has a broad, clear vision of the world panorama before him, yet in his clean, lofty air feels close to God. Is not a pontiff like that? He has a worldwide Church spread out before him, and in governing it he must always be close to the Christ whose place he takes.

Like Christ in Nazareth, Pius first worked in obscurity for a literal thirty years. Most of the time, Pius was a church librarian, "a mouse of the scrolls." He smoothed out yellow parchments, translated lines whose jet ink had stayed true through the centuries. That must have made a wincing memory later when he saw the paper of modern treaties fall apart almost before the ink was dry. But at this date he had no such international cares.

In the ranking of the Church, this spectacled figure — huddled over old manuscripts in the Milan Library — was only a priest. It seems remarkable that as late as his fifty-eighth year he was still a simple priest. Summoned to re-organize the Vatican Library, he advanced one notch to the grade of monsignor. "Monsignor" did not seem much of a consolation for the loss of the mountains of Milan. He was past sixty and apparently just an "extra" on the great Roman stage when the spotlight of fame first picked him out and brought him up front.

Somebody had recommended this avowed bookworm to the pope as the right man to represent him in Poland. Monsignor Ratti's own reaction was that he was the perfect misfit for a diplomatic assignment, and scholar-wise he listed the more obvious reasons. But when he was ushered into Pope Benedict's presence — and the latter opened the audience with, "Well, when are you leaving for Poland?" — Monsignor Ratti suddenly decided he was leaving at once, and the paper listing the reasons he shouldn't represent the pontiff crumpled in his moist fist.

So the man whose life had been spent between book-ends found himself wartime nuncio to Poland. He heard Bolshevik guns roaring only seven miles outside his residence in Warsaw. He watched other diplomats gather up their portfolios and flee for safety. Come what may, he told himself, he was going to stay. He did, and his presence was a tonic to the whole city's morale. Gradually, the Bolsheviks were pushed back. Poland later gave him the Order of the White Eagle.

From Warsaw he went back to Milan — but this time as Milan's cardinal-archbishop. The motto he chose for his coat of arms was meant to be humble with an ominous reminder of death: *"Raptim transit"* ("He passes quickly"). Instead it proved prophetic. In less than eight months Cardinal Ratti "passed" from Milan to Rome. He had been elected pope. Coronation Day was February 12, 1922, with silver trumpets blaring the papal fanfare from the balcony of Saint Peter's, the Sistine Choir thundering the processional sung only at the entrance of a pontiff: *"Tu es Petrus"* ("Thou art Peter"), and the Swiss Guard blazing in the striped uniform of red, yellow, and black designed by Michelangelo, with gleaming helmets and breastplates that had been passed down as heirlooms from father to son.

One of the very first pronouncements of the pontiff was a friendly gesture toward America. He felt chagrined that the papal elections were over before the American cardinals could arrive, and immediately enacted a ruling that henceforth balloting should not begin till at least fifteen days after the pope's death. There were other things too, trivial perhaps, but human things that linked Pius XI to America. He always shaved himself with an American safety razor. In a garage of luxurious foreign cars presented to him by automobile firms, he preferred his American-made 1929 Graham-Paige.

He beatified the first American citizen to receive that pre-saintly honor, Mother Cabrini. When a hundred or so midshipmen from Annapolis visited him during a cruise, he gave them a wholehearted welcome, so much so, that at the end of the audience a cheerleader stepped before the ranks of middies, called for three rousing "Navy's," and while the cheerleaders whirled handsprings, the corps thundered out the old football cheer so familiar to America's radio audiences. It ended with three staccato "Holy Father's." The Vatican was in consternation, majordomos gasped, Swiss Guards gripped halberds tighter, monsignors in billowing purple rushed into the chamber. Only the pope was calm and smiling. "Boys," he said, "please do it again."

America prides itself on its democratic form of government wherein the poorest may become president. Pius XI was born poor, born a peasant with generations of peasants behind him, born in a three-room tenement over a silk mill in an unheard-of village of Italy. The Lincoln saga of log cabin to White House is no more American in spirit than the rise of this peasant boy to pope and to the white cassock that symbolizes the spiritual leadership of some seven hundred million Catholics today. Pius XI had a tremendous admiration for American efficiency. From telephone system to library cabinets, he wanted the Vatican to have the latest and the best. His message was as old-fashioned as truth, but his method would be as modern as tomorrow afternoon. In his Vatican, only the works of art were medieval. He told the cardinals, "Some of you will fly to the next election of a pope, while I shall be winging my way in a different direction and by other means." A die-hard reactionary and slave of habit in at least one detail, he never filled but instead always dipped his fountain pen.

Pius XI enjoyed mountain-climber's health almost to the end of his eighty-one years. He seemed to put away sickness as a temptation. During the Holy Year he determined to let any pilgrim kiss his ring. When the year was over, the attendants had clicked off one million two hundred thousand people. He covered three or four really brisk miles circling his gardens every day. He suppressed the corps of papal physicians like a heresy. His contention was that one doctor was enough for one pope. And who should that doctor be but the board-of-health doctor of Vatican City! In 1936 the pontiff weakened noticeably but kept working hard as ever.

The cardinals were alarmed, and brave Cardinal Salotti volunteered to risk telling the energetic pope that he should take a long rest if he wanted to avoid an early collapse. Pius used only one sentence for rebuttal. "Salotti," he said icily, "God has endowed you with many talents, but He has denied you the clinical eye."

When the doctor prescribed a bloodletting to relieve his increasingly high blood pressure, the pope would not even set aside a special day. Whatever had to be done would have to be done the next day, between audiences. So, for one test, they punctured behind the ear, drained off the blood, and applied a gauze pad. After a while the pontiff put his handkerchief over the wound and resumed his schedule of audiences. Physicians shook their heads, editors prepared obituaries, and the pope began some new encyclicals.

But nature will not be downed. Pope Pius XI began to get paler, frailer, and, with his wan face and white soutane, looked (when he was nearing the end) like a figure carved in old ivory. The miracle is that his age had stood the burdens and sorrows of so long a reign. People saw the gold cross sparkling on his breast; they did not know it was burning into his heart. Russia and Bolshevism, Germany and Nazism, Mexico and its Communism, Italy and the Ethiopian War, Spain and its Civil War — they were all his

personal stations of the cross. He had his joys, it is true —
like the concordat that established the tiny Vatican State.
"The papacy wants independence, not territory." And
there was the liberating of "the Prisoner of the Vatican."
How could a free mountain spirit suffer himself or his successors to be caged?

But the interests of Pius XI were not just piled on Vatican Hill. He saw the world's wealth concentrated in the
hands of a few, and he flung his encyclicals like sticks of
dynamite into the midst of this evil. He saw that factories
had their slaves as much as the old galleys, and (like an
echo of Leo XIII) he trumpeted a call for labor to rally into
protective unions. He saw the insane theories of superior
race and the arrogant assumptions of a supreme state, and
he lashed out against both errors as champion of the in-
violable rights of the individual man.

And doing this, he died. The light that burned till after
midnight in the corner room on the third floor of the Vatican was at last out. It seemed very dark up there then, and
even darker down below. He died when we needed him
most. His highest tributes were the little expressions of sorrow that came spontaneously from the lips of common
men as they read that Friday's sad headline. A half-dozen
dictators would not be so genuinely mourned. We Catholics felt proud even in our sorrow. Best of all, we knew that
soon there would be another headline; soon God would
give us another guide. Peter was dead, Pius was dead —
but the pope lives on, the vicar of Christ, yesterday, today,
and the same forever!

{ John XXIII }

In recent times, the pope has always been a senior citizen.
But John XXIII was the oldest cardinal elected to the

papacy in two centuries. He was a venerable seventy-six. He took the name John, he said, in memory of his father, and then added with a twinkle in those brown eyes, "I have noticed from history that popes with that name have never been burdened with a long reign." History was right again. John XXIII reigned for only five years, 1958-1963.

His predecessor, Pius XII, whose pontificate lasted four times that long, was tall and slender like his crosier, and a scion of the old Roman nobility. John XXIII was portly in architecture and a peasant in family roots. Far from forgetting his modest origin, he delighted in bringing his rustic brothers to Rome from rural Bergamo. Cardinal Cushing used to say that he felt tense and strained in the presence of Pius XII but utterly relaxed with John XXIII. They recognized each other as kindred spirits, the one from South Boston and the other from an Italian village, but both buoyant spirits, dedicated to God and Church and happy in their commitment. Cardinal Cushing once said that John XXIII was the only high churchman who understood him. "And," he added with a shrug and a smile, "sometimes I don't understand myself."

When the college of cardinals chose John XXIII, they probably felt that they were electing an interim pope. At his advanced age John was supposed to be only a transitional pontiff, a temporary plugging of the leak with what was at hand till they could arrange for something solid and lasting. Pope John surprised them all by making history. He summoned the leaders of the entire Catholic world to the Second Vatican Council. Nothing in centuries would so change the Church.

The story got around, though no one ever claimed to have heard him say it, that one day Pope John had airily quipped, "I wanted to fling open a few windows around here and let in some fresh air." From that picturesque phrase it was only a small step, though on slippery rock, to make John into an ecclesiastical revolutionary. But anyone who reads Pope John's *Journey of a Soul* knows that this is continents away from the dull but sturdy truth.

This churchman was so conservative and traditional in his own spiritual life that he said the whole fifteen decades of the beads every day. This and reciting the Breviary and making a visit to the Blessed Sacrament — all these were musts in his daily schedule. While he surprised the world by giving the best seats at the Second Vatican Council to the non-Catholic observers, he let it be known that there was only one true Church. He wanted to let everyone know that the purpose of ecumenism was to speak the words of truth in tones of love, that Catholic and Protestant were not blended together indiscernibly like eggs in an omelette. They were together only like slices of apple and orange and bananas and cherry in a fruit salad. They were together, but they were different. Christ had founded only one Church.

Warm and cordial as an open fire, he loved all people as children of God. He must have winked when he visited the jails of Rome and said, "Since you could not come to see me, I have come to see you." He never forgot that the word "papal," with its overtones of solemn dignity and colorful pageantry, came from *papa,* the Latin diminutive for "father." On his deathbed he said, "I offer my sufferings for all my fellowmen, black, white, brown, any color."

The pope who was supposed to preside over a Church which for a few years would merely mark time marched forward as no pope before him had dared. John XXIII created the first black, Japanese, and Filipino cardinals. He said that God, with all His perfections, suffered from one defect: He was color-blind.

Yet he knew that each nation had its own culture and its own language, and so made that monumental change by which the Mass was no longer said in Latin but in the vernacular, the language of the people. Communion would be the same for all, but communication would change with the flag.

He never considered even the possibility of women as members of the priesthood, but he always insisted that the moral future of any country lay in the hands of its wives and mothers.

Like many plump people, he was naturally jolly. A shrewd peasant sense of humor often crinkled his round face into a merry smile. When as patriarch of Venice he blessed vineyards, where the grapes hung in fat purple bunches, he said, "You must send me some of your wine. With all this water around us, we need wine." When someone asked him how many people worked in the Vatican he said dryly, "About half." When photographers exploded their flashbulbs in his face, he shook his head and smilingly said, "There are fourteen works of mercy, seven corporal and seven spiritual. But there should be fifteen: one for putting up with the people that annoy us."

Before his pontificate the pope had always dined alone in his absolutely off-limits private dining room. John XXIII first brought his family there, in their crude country suits and gingham dresses, and eventually clerical and lay friends. He said, "When I dine alone I feel like a seminarian being punished."

You might even say that this pope canonized Saint Joseph. To canonize basically means to insert the name of that saint in the Canon of the Mass. Now we call the Canon the Eucharistic Prayer. Although several obscure Roman martyrs had always been invoked in the Canon, curiously, Saint Joseph never was. During Vatican II, John XXIII made the first change in the Canon in about four hundred years by including the name of Joseph. He is there today in the first of the four Eucharistic Prayers.

Other popes in recent times had been admired for

their learning, like Leo XIII, or admired for their holiness, like Pius X. But this man was more than admired — he was loved by the whole world. He came across not as a stiff and solemn prelate but as a warm man of God. When he was dying he said, "My bags are packed. I am ready to go." He knew he loved God and he hoped that God loved him.

To the first pope, Peter, our Lord had said, "To thee I give the keys of the kingdom." To this pope He surely said, "To thee I give the kingdom of the keys!"

c h a p t e r   t w o

ON THIS ROCK

{ Catacomb to Cathedral }

These days you can hardly pick up a Catholic paper without reading something that leaves you puzzled, bewildered, alarmed, irritated, disturbed, chagrined, infuriated, or depressed. A good remedy for this might be to open a book of history. Here it dawns on you that through the centuries, kings and crowns and scepters and thrones have reached their golden peak of glory, and then gradually, or sometimes even suddenly, have fallen away into mere fragments of history.

Yet all this time the long white line of the popes marches steadily on. There was a pope in the fourth century to crown the Emperor Constantine. There was a pope in the ninth century to crown the Emperor Charlemagne. There was a pope in the nineteenth century to crown the Emperor Napoleon. The Church has been around a long time.

But put down the calendar and take up the map. If you hear Mass in some dilapidated chapel on the slopes of the Andes, or in the majestic cathedral of Chartres (whose gorgeous stained-glass windows make you think you are standing inside a giant rainbow jewel), you attend the same holy sacrifice. If you go to confession in Venice, near the Grand Canal, or in Newfoundland, off the Grand Banks, it is the same reconciling sacrament.

For the moment, however, think not of the unity of worship but of the difference of worshipers. Is there any other human community that gathers under the same universal canopy so many millions who by their origins and temperaments, their backgrounds and their cultures, are so different? They are all Catholics: the reserved Englishman and the vivacious Frenchman; the methodical German and the warm Italian; the serious Slav and the smiling, happy-go-lucky Irishman.

This, mind you, is the crew of the Ship of Peter, the Church. It is a motley, mixed-up crew, and by all human standards the Church with such a crew should have long since gone gurgling down to the bottom. It should have become just another of the has-beens of history. Except for one thing: Christ was aboard! The Christ who said, "I shall be with you all days, even to the consummation of the world."

Is it not true that in its very infancy that Church should have been crushed between the military might of the Roman Empire and the religious prestige of the Jewish synagogue, as easily as a butterfly under a sledge hammer? But somehow it wasn't.

Not long afterward, the barbarian invasions came swooping down on the young Church, like a cloud of locusts on a spring garden. That should have been the end of the Church: brutal devastation. But somehow it wasn't.

Later came the scarlet-and-gold age of the Renaissance, the era of worldly cardinals with their pagan art and sometimes dissolute lives. This should have been the end of the Church: cancer from within. But strangely, it wasn't.

Then came the Reformation, when overnight a half-dozen nations broke off from the Church like branches from the vine. This should have been the end of the Church: disintegration. But strangely, somehow it wasn't.

Fast upon that came the so-called Age of Reason,

when divine revelation was dropped gingerly into the wastebasket, and philosophers like Voltaire flung the whistling stones of their mockeries through every stained-glass window of doctrine in the cathedral of the Church. This should have been the end of the Church: direct intellectual assault. But strangely, it wasn't.

Why, you may ask, wasn't it the end? It is because the Church is not stained-glass windows or statues. It is not bell, book, and candle. It is not vestments and incense. The Church essentially is Christ, the current, contemporary, living Christ. The Christ who said, "I shall be with you all days." Christ still teaching, Christ still preaching, Christ still forgiving, Christ still suffering. Above all, still suffering!

During the Second Vatican Council, an aged bishop from Yugoslavia shuffled up to the podium and, in a weak, quavering voice, appealed to the assembled bishops to include the name of Saint Joseph in the Canon of the Mass. To the vast majority this request at that moment seemed unimportant. They were concerned with major changes, like the Mass in English and that kind of thing. So they expressed disapproval in the routine fashion of slapping the bench. Imagine about fifteen hundred palms (with rings yet!), pounding in unison to the chant, *"Non ad rem! Non ad rem!"* ("Not to the point! Not to the point!")

The old bishop backed off and tottered to his place. At the end of that particular morning's session, the presiding cardinal finished the customary prayer with an almost sarcastic, "Saint Joseph, pray for us!" And everybody smiled.

But back in the Vatican, Pope John (who watched all the proceedings on closed-circuit TV) did not smile. He knew that this old bishop had been imprisoned for nine years in a Communist jail. He knew that the Communists had contrived an accident in which the aged prelate had

33

broken both his legs, and that he had been left for eighteen hours without any medical attention. All the time the agonizing bishop prayed to Saint Joseph.

The very next day, Pope John made the first change in the Canon of the Mass in centuries. He ordered the inclusion of the name of Joseph, just as it appears in our first canon today. When the Council Fathers learned the whole story, naturally they were a bit abashed, and began to wonder how many among them still bore on their bodies the scars of Communism. How many were there: thirty, forty? No matter. On many attending the Council, this incident left the deepest impression of all.

The Apostle Thomas recognized Christ by His wounds. And by the scarlet wounds of persecution on the Mystical Body of Christ, and the long red line of the Church's martyrs — is it not by this that we too recognize the Savior, still suffering in our midst?

Because the Church was founded by Christ (who is God) upon Peter (who was the Rock), the Church is divine in its origin, and everlasting in its destiny. But, like the Blessed Sacrament, which begins with ordinary bread, the Church is composed of ordinary people and ordinary things. People as far apart as saints and sinners; things as different as Scriptures and scapulars, miters and medals, sacraments and sacramentals; truths that come directly from God and that never can be changed, and legislation that comes from the Church ("He who hears you, hears Me") and can be changed tomorrow. For example, the Church can never go back on the Real Presence of our Lord in Holy Communion; but the Church could change at any time how long we have to fast, or whether we have to fast at all, to receive our Lord eucharistically.

But the Church is more than legislation, more than canons, more than rubrics. Do you know what the Church is? It is the great army of believers marching along the pilgrim path toward heaven. It is the huge, monumental dome of Saint Peter's in Rome, and the graceful Gothic spires of Saint Patrick's in New York. But it is also the weather-beaten clapboard church on the plains of Kansas, and the bush chapel with a thatched roof and a cross of twigs in deepest Africa.

It is a May procession of little girls with lacy veils and silvery voices, and it is the grimmer procession of a prison chaplain and a felon, walking with faltering steps toward the gas chamber. It is holy water glistening on an open grave, and it is vigil lights fluttering like flowers in front of a Marian shrine.

It is a chalice of gold encrusted with diamonds, raised before a marble cathedral altar. And it is the tiny egg-cup chalice lifted secretly in a log cabin in a Siberian concentration camp. It is the wealthy lady who walks in swirls of perfume and gives generous gifts to the Church, and it is the Little Sister of the Poor who gives God only her life.

It is a row of seven-year-olds, ranged at the altar rail like a row of lilies, to receive their Lord for the first time. And it is the priest bending over the mangled figure on the highway to administer the last rites while the approaching ambulance blinks and screams in the distance.

It is the Angelus bell swinging in the steeple, the word of God ringing from the pulpit, the whispering of faults and falls in the confessional, the feeble whimper of a tiny new Christian under the waters of baptism. It is even the quavering notes of an ancient soprano in the parish choir at the Christmas Midnight Mass.

It is Ash Wednesday and Holy Thursday and Palm Sunday. It is you and I, and seven hundred million like us, who believe the same truths, receive the same sacraments, and obey the same spiritual head, the admittedly human John Paul II, who gets his authority from the very human Peter, who got his authority from the divine Jesus Christ.

When you hear pessimists groaning about the sad state of the Church, just remember it has weathered far fiercer storms. When you hear of priests and nuns leaving the Church and gloomily forecasting its imminent end (and their words sound like gravel rattling down on a rough box at an old-time funeral), just remember that the Church will never be buried. Originally it was planted! Planted by Christ, protected by heaven, pruned in grim days like these of its unworthy members, it will go on living, nourished by the bones of its enemies, and alas, even of some of its unworthy caretakers.

It all moves the thinking man more solemnly to say:

"This is the faith I have held, and hold.

And this is that in which I mean to die."

} Follow the Pope! {

During the 1960s liberal Catholics did not throw up their hats and cheer wildly for Pope Paul VI. He had stepped front and center into the spotlight and said some stern things about sacerdotal celibacy and some stern things about matrimonial contraception, so he was not a popular pope. But John XXIII, when he came on the scene, ah, here was something else! Here was a true forward-looker, a progressive, a modern.

Was he, though? John XXIII, warm and genial and portly, was "out in front" only in his personal architecture. Actually he was a confirmed traditionalist, a "rosary Catholic." And not just five decades, mind you. He said the whole fifteen decades every day.

If you read his *Journey of a Soul*, or his encyclical *Mater et Magistra*, you realize that this man could never abide any essential change in the age-old teachings of the Church. What he wanted from Vatican II was simply to present the old truths in a new, modern package. But when you read some recent Catholic literature you wonder if you are reading right. Here writers wonder about the Real Presence, conjecture about the Virgin Birth, interpret the Resurrection, and even condone premarital sex as long as it represents true love.

Take the statues out of the churches, bring far-out catechisms in, and if you should demur at all this, you are hopelessly medieval or at least pathetically Tridentine. A theological Neanderthal! And all this breaking-away from the anchored doctrines of the past is made in the name of Vatican II! Before you swallow it, pause to hear Paul VI lay it on the line: "Those people would be mistaken who think that the Council represents a break from, or as some would have it, a liberation from the traditional teachings of the Church."

This seems clear enough, and if you wonder why there is confusion, consider the comment of that late ecclesiastical luminary Cardinal Wright, who said, "The clear fixed stars of the Catholic faith are momentarily obscured by theological smog."

During Vatican II the Church was like a ship being overhauled and refitted in drydock. The same ship returned to the water with a crashing splash and is still quivering. It will take a little time to steady itself and sweep forward. Before Vatican II most Protestant sects envied the Catholic Church its solid unity. A few bitterly opposed its confident, forthright claims. But even the most hostile respected it because here was a force that knew where it stood and what it stood for. From the red dawn of history the Church had been a fortress of undoubted and unshaken faith.

But now — after Vatican II — the picture has changed. Keep in mind that *after* Vatican II, not *because of* Vatican II, confessions began falling off, as did conversions, Mass attendance, and parish missions. The once radiant image of the priesthood has dimmed, and its ranks have thinned. Convent doors have swung open as nuns left in droves, and parish school doors have banged closed as children went to school elsewhere. Among the laity, particularly the young, there has been much confusion.

Is this, one timidly wonders, the great renewal, the glorious sunrise of a revived faith that was supposed to spread across the Catholic world after Vatican II? If not, why not? Consider just one melancholy item in our litany of lamentations: Why are confessions down? Is it because fewer sins are being committed, or is it because fewer sins are being admitted? Is it not because our sense of sin, the stark reality of guilt, is (in certain quarters) being diluted and diminished? Are not some priests and nuns in their teaching deliberately downplaying the need of confession?

But when you want to establish the Church's stand on confession, do you go to some callow curate who at the moment is hungrier for publicity than for Paradise, or to some avant-garde nun who has become dizzy with her newfound freedom, or do you go to headquarters, the top? "Avant-garde" means out front, leading; but the only one who has a God-given right to be out there leading and guiding is our Holy Father, the pope. With him you will find no downgrading of confession.

Liberal Catholics would attract no attention whatever by their statements if they left the Church and flung their radical comments from the outside. Surely the Church, since it is made up not of archangels or seraphs but of human beings, is going to have faults. But for someone who calls himself a Catholic to concentrate on these faults is like standing on a housetop and shouting out your family's shortcomings to the neighborhood. It is like hiring a billboard to insult your mother. Is not such conduct outrageous, and stupid?

Those in the media, of course, live by news. News is the new, the unusual, the unexpected, the different. It focuses on the one West Point cadet out of step on the parade grounds. Everybody takes for granted the rhythm of the regiment. This is not news. The cameras and the headlines are greedy for the flaw. "Ten Commandments" and "Seven Sacraments" will never make the papers. "Seven Commandments" and "Ten Sacraments" would rate an extra edition.

Let a hundred good priests in any ordinary big city go about their ordinary daily duties, saying Mass, preaching sermons, baptizing babies, hearing confessions, visiting the sick, praying the Breviary and the rosary, and the media will merely yawn. But if five or six priests slip into City Hall to get married, then watch out! Stop the presses! Heighten and widen the headlines!

In the same way, in the old days when people lined up for confession, this never rated even a lone reporter; but let one splinter group gather for a general absolution without confession, and look for exploding flashbulbs. In any unusual occurrence in the Church, ask yourself just one question: Does this have the approbation of the official Church and the pope? If it does not, take it with a whole barrel of salt.

Never tie your faith to the trial balloon of some venturesome theologian. This is not to put down all theologians, period. Most of them are competent and holy men. They write their profound articles. They deliver their learned addresses. They fill a definite niche in the cathedral of doctrine. In spiritual research they can light a match and illuminate a corner hitherto obscure. They can lift an edge of the veil and call attention to something previously overlooked. By doing this they have made monumental contributions to our religious knowledge. For this they deserve and receive our absorbed attention, our ungrudging admiration, our spontaneous gratitude.

Give them appreciation and thanks by the bushelful; but we can never give them — these theologians and religious writers — faith. To no theologian, not even to Saint Thomas Aquinas, was there ever given a guarantee against error. Never to any theologian but only to Peter and the Apostles did our Blessed Lord say, "I will be with you all days, even to the end of the world." Not the theologians but the pope, and the bishops with the pope, are therefore the successors of Peter and the Apostles; thus Christ is with them. These, and not the theologians, are our guides as we march along the path of faith, and our guardians so that we do not stray.

Theologians can suggest; the Church teaches. Theologians can offer opinions; the Church lays down doctrines. Theologians may present theories; the Church announces truths. Only the Church is the legitimate channel of faith, and only to the Church did Christ say, "He who hears you, hears me." If you want the real doctrine, hold on to the Church and the teaching of the head of the Church, the Holy Father. Put your hand into the hand of the man whose hand goes back in an unbroken chain of hands to the hand of Peter and the fingertips of Jesus Christ. In three blunt, simple, straight words: "Follow the pope!"

c h a p t e r   t h r e e

BASIC MORALITY

{ Supernatural Supermarket }

When Mary, the housewife of Nazareth, wanted bread, she could scarcely drop into a neighborhood store and pick up a loaf that was wrapped in cellophane and mathematically sliced. Mary had to bake her own bread. When she wanted vegetables, she had to depend on the little truck garden behind the little stone cottage or hope for the peddler's cart that would come creaking through the village. When she wanted milk, it came from a cow owned in common by a few families. (That milk was not pasteurized, only "pasturized.") There was no refrigeration, so meat came from a lamb or calf recently butchered and sold to several buyers. Coffee, tea, and sugar were unheard-of luxuries.

The modern American housewife, on the contrary, can find all these things and so much more under one roof (if her purse is first cousin to Fort Knox) in that marvel of modern merchandising we call the supermarket. What will you have: spinach or spaghetti, sardines or saltines? Here they are! Come down this beautiful aisle of cereals, and you will find cereals that snap and pop and crackle, and other cereals that just lie on your plate and stare up at you sullenly. Potatoes from Idaho, ham from Iowa, coffee from Colombia, bananas from Guatemala, tuna fish from Samoa — they are all here. It is as if the *National Geographic* magazine had married a cookbook and this is the savory offspring.

But more than that. The supermarket has overtones of the supernatural, or at least of the spiritual, the moral. Do you know how the supermarket began? With the art or the science of packaging. Some of us can remember back to World War I, and the days of the neighborhood grocer's. There was the open sugar barrel with its crusted scoop, the open candy barrel with its sticky lumps, the open cracker barrel with its crumbly cookies. And overhead, in warm weather, the flies. They droned near the ceiling in lazy circles, skidding in every few minutes to refuel at the sugar or the candy or the cookies.

Then came packaging and cellophane, and everything was boxed up, glassed in, sealed off. The pertinent question is: Do they think more of the cleanliness of their merchandise than we do of the cleanliness of our minds? All around us, buzzing like flies, are temptations, whispers of evil, suggestions of sin. We live in an age of ancient paganism with modern plumbing. Anyone who thinks that these days he can read any book he chooses, see any movies he wants, attend any party he cares to, is likely to find that the soul can sour faster than whipped cream left in the sun.

To survive clean we have to make of our soul a prayer package by immediately turning from temptation and turning toward God — the oldest recipe in spirituality. Only by doing this can anyone survive unstained in a corrupt world.

But the supermarket is not only clean, it is also attractive. That is why someone may go there intending to pick up some cornflakes or hamburgers and be tempted to include some pickled onions or salted almonds or crabmeat. But it is not a question of what we would like to have, but what we can afford to buy.

In life too there is the same problem. The shelves of temptation are attractive too, otherwise we would not be drawn to them. But here the question is, not what we have an inclination for, but what we have a right to. Here we look not at our cash but at our conscience. In the supermarket it is "shelf control." In life it is self-control.

In the supermarket, beneath the bundle of asparagus tips or the box of blueberry muffins there is a little white card with a little black number: the price. It is the same way in the moral world. If we reach beyond our right in a serious matter, it is clearly marked that it is a serious sin, a mortal sin. This means the immediate, automatic loss of God's friendship, the metaphorical ugly stain on the soul, and (should we die in that state) a stern judgment and an everlasting hell. The price is not right. The price is far too high!

Every now and then supermarkets revive an ancient gimmick called trading stamps. There are green stamps, gold stamps (perhaps even zebra stamps or polka-dotted stamps). These can turn people from customers into stamp collectors. A bargain day can become a stampede. Consider the woman who was clearly heard saying to her friend at the exit of a supermarket: "I know I shouldn't have bought this pineapple pie. But they were offering one hundred stamps!"

Isn't this a case of the tail wagging the dog? Is not the premium here more important than the product? Some deluded souls go through life in this manner, with their values turned upside down. They are so concerned with superficial things like bridge scores and hairdos and batting averages and recipes and the like that they completely forget the supernatural things like the soul and God and the hereafter.

Their life is like a charm bracelet, tinkling with trifles. They never face the towering questions: Why am I here? Where am I headed? How do I stand at this moment with God? Certainly we have to make a living, but we must never forget the main purpose of life: to save our immortal soul.

Against all this consider the man who in the course of his life achieved financial success, social prestige, political power, but somewhere along the way mislaid God. And, curiously, he is apparently well pleased with himself. Is he not like someone who is delighted in finding a tin whistle in a box of Cracker Jacks, while at the same time losing the pearl of great price, his soul?

Somehow it brings to mind the encounter of two saints, Ignatius of Loyola and Francis Xavier, at the University of Paris, now the Sorbonne. Young Francis Xavier had everything. From a wealthy family, he had money. Of noble stock, he was heir to a title. Physically he was tall, athletic, an excellent boxer, and a super swordsman. But he was a bit worldly. Ignatius Loyola, a sore-legged soldier, lately returned from the wars, limped into the university to study Latin and become a priest. Whenever he ran across Francis, the young professor, he would smile and say, "What does it profit?" Francis knew the rest: "What does it profit a man if he gain the whole world and lose his soul — forever?"

One evening Francis, just finishing the correction of some class papers, thought of Ignatius, and idly wrote on the paper 1,000,000 — to indicate a million years. He added three more ciphers, a billion; then three more, a trillion. A trillion years! The head reels trying to comprehend a trillion years. Francis glanced at the point of his quill. There was still ink on it. What figure could he write without even dipping again? And what figure could he write with all the ink in the bottle? How many years in there?

Francis sauntered over to the window where the River Seine slid past, sluggish and black like ink. If this *were* ink, what figure could he write? And suppose the Atlantic were ink, and the Pacific, and all the waters of the world . . . if they were ink, what incredible number of years could one put down? But no matter what number, eventually it would end, because it was finite. But eternity, being infinite, would never end. This chilling thought made Francis Xavier decide to save his own soul — forever — and to plead with others to save their souls. With this message, he became the most famous of all foreign missionaries.

Speaking of saving one's soul, that line of gleaming wire carts in the supermarket stands like a silent sermon on salvation. How? Well, in a supermarket you can consult a clerk in this department or that; but, by and large, on the average trip you don't consult anybody. *You* take the macaroni or the macaroons off the shelf, *you* drop them in the cart, *you* wheel the cart down the aisle. *You* negotiate the transaction.

Isn't it the same in life? Preachers may thunder at you, confessors may whisper to you, friends may plead with you, nuns may pray for you; but, in the last analysis, you save your own soul. Salvation is strictly a solo proposition.

One last thing. In a supermarket, as you go through, you can take what you want. Your eye roams the glamorous shelves, your hand reaches out, you toss the article into your cart — any article. But as you leave, when you come to the check-out counter, there stands a character with an iceberg heart, a lightning eye, and rippling fingers, who taps out the tab. You pay as you leave.

Isn't it this way with life too? As we go through life we can break God's commandments like peanut brittle. We can blow away the laws of the Church like cigarette smoke. But just as we leave, at the check-out counter of death, we encounter not a clerk but Christ. He looks not at our cart but at our conscience, our soul. We pay as we leave.

Does this sound morbid, macabre, grim? It should not. If we sincerely do our best, faithfully say our prayers, regularly receive the sacraments, doggedly keep the Ten

Commandments, we are walking the right road. On that road sometimes we may stumble, even fall; but as long as we do not stay down but struggle to our feet, we are stumbling toward heaven. Our Lord is more willing to forgive than we can be to ask forgiveness. Perhaps He chose to die on the cross so that we might have in the crucifix a symbol of arms outstretched to the sinner in everlasting welcome!

{ Family Unit }

If you do not believe that we live in a weird world, consider this. The dictionary on my desk, if you turn to the word *family*, lists only as its fifth meaning, "Parents and children living under the same roof." The first meaning is "Fellowship." Where has sanity fled?

The family is founded on nature, and nature begins with God. Pick up an ashtray, cup, or the like, and turn it over. Read the name of the country where it was made: Japan, Korea, Czechoslovakia. But the family was molded by the fingertips of the Almighty. It is not an artificial arrangement like the Boston Birdwatchers or the Mormon Tabernacle Choir. It is not a club, not a corporation, not a conglomerate. It goes all the way back to the pink dawn of creation.

Not only did the Almighty create the family Himself, He paid it His highest compliment when His only Son joined one. Our Blessed Lord had His whole mission to prepare for, namely the redemption of mankind. Yet He did not get ready by living as a hermit on a hilltop, or as a prophet in a remote desert. For nine tenths of His life, Jesus lived under a family roof, and only then went forth to His preaching and His miracles and gory death.

In doing this, was not our Blessed Lord showing His

high esteem of family life? The world honors engineers for their towering bridges, artists for their glowing canvases, authors for their learned books, sculptors for their graceful statues. Yet parents work in the family circle not with stone or steel or canvas but with immortal souls. All the rest — stone and steel and canvas — will eventually and inevitably crumble, but the soul of every child is forever!

To a celibate priest who observes the life of his brothers or sisters (and, as he grows older, his nephews and nieces), the rearing of a family is almost an awesome proposition. He bows his head, in admiration, to dedicated parents. Who can count the work and the worries, the backaches and the headaches and (alas!) the heartaches, as a devoted mother and father bring their little ones through babyhood on to childhood, then through those teenage years when the boy or girl walks that treacherous, teetering tightrope between boyhood or girlhood and maturity?

Many a parent, looking back, must marvel how it was done. Consider just the material side. Think of all the supermarket carts filled with cornflakes or hamburgers, cans of soup, ears of corn, loaves of bread, everything and anything. For how many years, for so many hours, sometimes working two jobs, the father of the family has had to work to put the meals on the table! Think too of the tower of dishes rising through the years that the mother has washed, all the beds she has made, all the hills of potatoes (if they were piled together) that she has peeled!

Not to forget the work and the sacrifices that go to clothing a family, from snowsuits to bathing suits, and the footwear that goes all the way from woolly baby booties to size elevens for the high-school halfback's shoes that look like landing barges. And don't overlook the thousand concerns about health: tonsils, teeth, mumps and measles, a broken arm, a tense bout with pneumonia, the anxious hours, the sleepless nights — perhaps even a dark tragedy.

But family life is a plaid, and there are bright colors too, like the birthdays with their cakes and presents, Christmas with its merry glow, Easter with its golden joy and bright new outfits. Just about then may come the nagging worry about one child who has been a bit slow in school. Then, all the helping with the homework, and the exams and the prayers and the vigil lights: "Dear God, please let Georgianna pass her geometry!"

From the sidelines any thoughtful priest looking at the rearing of children, which is what a family is all about, has to remove his hat in a sweeping bow and salute the often heroic devotion of mothers and fathers. These parents are the Church of today, and they are training the Church of tomorrow. The words and example of father and mother have more impact on the children than the Church or the school can ever have. It is the home that makes the child.

The influence of a good mother and father is sometimes a delayed-action agent. How often you see a teenager turn delinquent for a few years, and then level off to become a respectable, responsible adult, because all the past training of family life begins to rise, like sap in a tree after winter, and the individual responds to the life and memory of good God-fearing parents!

Your average devoted father and mother not only would give their lives for their children, but all along the way they are giving their lives to their children. The children along the way: the wee ones who give you a laugh an hour and a scare a day; the growing ones who never go out without slamming a door; the grown ones — and before you know it the tiny lad with his first curl is the tall young fellow with his first girl. Perhaps this is the hardest time of all, when they want to slip in the house so quietly (no slamming of doors now) that you will not hear them at all. Then you wonder if your work has been worthwhile. Have they learned the lessons you tried to teach about self-control and purity and honor and all the rest? From the high chair to the wheelchair the problems of life march grimly on!

But there is always help, God's own supernatural help, His all-powerful grace. Our Blessed Lord not only once sanctified the family by becoming a member of a family Himself, but He continues to offer special help to families through His grace-bearing sacraments. Every Catholic family begins when the bridal couple marches under the sacred arch of the sacrament of matrimony. This is not a conclusion; it is a beginning. From now on they have a right to tap that sacrament of matrimony for all the graces they need during their married lives.

Should God bless the couple with children, there is a special sacrament to welcome and sanctify each. We call it baptism; and when the bright waters flow over the tiny brow, that child automatically becomes a child of God and an heir to the kingdom of heaven.

And so the family sacraments march on: confession, to sponge away the grimy guilt of faults; Holy Communion, to unite all members in the same Eucharist, all joined with the one great Father, God.

In another less sacred sense, parents can say of their child, "This is my body. This is my blood." But now that child walks from the first communion altar with the Body and Blood of Christ within him or her, and more worthy to contain that Body and Blood than the most precious chalice in Christendom!

With adolescence comes the sacrament of confirmation whereby the growing youngster is strengthened in the Catholic faith. Should serious illness lay its pale hand upon the child, there is the sacrament of the anointing of the sick. And so life comes full circle to that happy day when wedding bells ring in their tower for the son or daughter, or perhaps the sanctuary bell tinkles at the first Mass of a new priest.

How strange it is that some otherwise exemplary fathers and mothers wince at the thought of their children becoming priests or nuns or brothers! How depressing the findings of the questionnaire that revealed that six out of every ten seminarians, and seven out of every ten nuns, had encountered opposition in their own home when they wished to heed the call of Christ.

Is it really a Catholic family if it so callously stands in God's way? Where are the priorities, the sense of values? God does not knock at every door. If He knocks at yours, let Him in! If He wants one of your family to work shoulder to shoulder with His own Son in His cause, He is honoring your house. Don't slam the door! Our Lady said "Yes" and gave the world its first Priest and our Savior. The family that gives a son or daughter to God will be blessed a hundredfold.

The family that is united in the love and service of God will be a happy family. Not perhaps a rich family, but a basically happy one. There will be inevitable little tiffs, and some stepping on a few toes, and occasional flare-ups; but these troubles will be splinters and not planks. The family that is faithful to the laws of God and His Church will get the graces to carry it over the rough spots.

There is a story about a lad who complained to his father that the latter had forgotten to bring him a jigsaw puzzle. Dad grunted and noticed that one whole page of the newspaper he was reading featured a map of the world. So, while the boy watched, he tore the map into strips and pieces, thrust them into the boy's hand and said, "Here, put this together." In a surprisingly short time the boy was back, the puzzle all laid out on a desk blotter. The father was amazed. "How did you do it so fast?" he asked. "Well, I noticed that when you began to tear up the map, on the side facing me was a full-page, life-size photo of a family. So I went to work on the family, and I found that when I had the family straightened out, the world took care of itself."

It will too.

} Holocaust of the Unborn {

Ten years after the Supreme Court's open season on the unborn by sanctioning abortion, a nationally known hospital within the confines of our parish offered abortions over the weekend. At the opposite end of the parish another hospital, also of national stature, offered abortions to adolescents from twelve to seventeen. Is it not about time that we rose up in decent indignation?

It is true that the Supreme Court has made abortion legal. But no Supreme Court can ever make abortion moral. They will tell you, of course, that since the Court has spoken, the Church should remain quiet. They will tell you that abortion is a medical matter, or a social matter, not a religious matter. Certainly not a Catholic matter. And here how precisely right they are! For when did Christ found His Church? Less than two thousand years ago. But abortion was wrong long before that. It was wrong back in the days of Abraham and Isaac and Jacob, long before there ever was a Catholic Church.

True, the Catholic Church opposes and condemns abortion. But it also condemns larceny, bribery, perjury. These crimes are not wrong because the Catholic Church condemns them. The Catholic Church condemns them because they are wrong. There is in each of them, as in abortion, something intrinsically, essentially, wrong.

What then is precisely wrong about abortion? Only this: It is the direct, deliberate, voluntary killing of an in-

51

nocent human life. Certainly everyone admits that what is destroyed in an abortion is living, that there is life. Certainly too that this life is innocent. What crime has it committed? Whom has it injured? Clearly, then, the only possible arguable word is human.

But how can there be any dispute about that? When you began to be in your mother's womb, did you start off as some kind of plant life? Were you a species of fish or fowl or some fur-bearing animal? Did you then, in the course of nine months, make an incredible change from the nonhuman to the human? If you did, you have overturned all the laws of evolution, which would demand not months but ages for such a transformation.

More than that. By this change from nonhuman to human you go counter to the whole genetic code. In layman's language this means that whatever you were when you emerged from the womb, you had been that from the very beginning. There were then locked in your first chromosomes the color of your eyes, the tint of your hair, your tendency to be tall or short, all your personal characteristics. You were *you* from the start. After the start you merely developed. Nothing was added. You only progressed or developed, as a child of one develops into the man or woman of twenty-one.

Most people are surprised to learn how quickly the human being does develop even in the earliest stages. Thirty days after conception, the kidneys, the liver, and the spinal column are discernible. This means that by the time a woman suspects that she is pregnant, and goes to the doctor and has the laboratory tests, all these organs are already there.

Most abortions take place after the second month. But by ten weeks the tiny fingers and toes are clearly recognizable. You ask: How could any mother, could she see this, bring herself to destroy it? Destroy is almost too kind a word. It does not emphasize the curette that savagely scrapes away life, or the saline solution that sends that life into convulsions before death, or the vacuum suction pump that disintegrates it. Could any mother bring any of this home and live with it?

When it is done, if conscience be not dead, how terrible the remorse! You try to assure such a mother, when the wickedness of it prostrates her, that God forgives. And it is true. God will forgive even murder, whether the victim is thirty years old in a living room or thirty days old in a womb. God will forgive, but how hard it is for the mother to forget! For how many years will that little baby's face peer at her through the window of her heart?

Some, of course, will sniff disdainfully that this is being ultradramatic, because what was killed was not really a baby but only the blueprint of a baby. Blueprint? You can take the blueprint of a future building and lay it on a desk and leave it there till the blueprint fades into yellow, and that blueprint will never develop into steel girders and concrete walls and bright windows and a new building. But just leave that so-called blueprint of a baby alone where it belongs, in the mother's womb, and in normal circumstances it will develop into a person. Blueprint?

Or they may tell you that, strictly speaking, the child has no real right to life because at that time it cannot exist independently of the mother. In order to live, it has to be within the mother. But take an infant six months old and put it in the hills outside the city, and tell me how long that child will continue to live on its own. As a matter of fact the child within the womb is less exposed to danger or disease than the child outside the womb.

Or, they will insist (and this is supposed to be their trump card) that it is the *mother's* body and over that body she has complete control. It is *her* body, so she has absolute dominion over it. Has she? Let her try to commit suicide a couple of times, attempting to destroy that body, and see how quick the state will put her in a padded cell. The whole point here is that the fetus, if you want to use that word, while it certainly is *in* the mother's body is just as certainly not part of the mother's body. An appendix there, about to rupture, would surely be part of the mother's body because it has the same cell structure as the mother's body. But the embryo or the fetus in the womb has a completely different cell pattern and is a completely different individual. For example, while the mother is female, the child could be male. The mother could be white and the child black. The mother may be backward and dull; the child may be almost a genius. They are two entirely different people.

Or they will shout that abortion is a totally private affair. Up to our time abortion has always been a secret affair, because it was always a shameful affair. Something done furtively in the dark, something that cannot stand the light. People boast of their operations. Did you ever hear anyone boasting of an abortion?

This brings up the matter of the so-called therapeutic abortion where the child is killed to save the mother's life. It is easy to see how some people could go along with this in good faith, because it would be better to have one death than two. But it is never — repeat, *never* — lawful under God to take an innocent life even to save another life. Medically that dilemma hardly ever exists. Therapeutic abortion is poor medicine.

By the way, do you know how many abortions are performed to save the mother's life? In every hundred abortions, about two. The other ninety-eight abortions are abortions of convenience. The child is just not wanted.

When the U.S. Supreme Court allowed two people, a woman and a doctor, to decide — without a hearing, without appeal — whether another human being should live or die, it was wearing its black judicial robes. It should have been wearing a hangman's black mask. In so decreeing, the Supreme Court was turning its back on the tradition of civilization and on the statutes of all the individual states.

Suppose on that day there had been present in the courtroom some of our country's Founding Fathers, like Washington or Jefferson or Adams. Suppose that they had heard the decision, "Abortion approved!" Would the Founding Fathers have been surprised? I do not think so. Surprised? A supermarket would surprise them. A color television screen would astonish them. A trip to the moon would astound them. But to hear that abortion (in their day a felonious crime) is suddenly declared legal and respectable — this would have shocked them right down to their shoe buckles. These were the men who fought for life, liberty, and the pursuit of happiness. But how can you have life if you do not have the right to be born?

The Supreme Court that allowed abortion is the same Supreme Court that decided in the Dred Scott case that a black man did not have the rights of a citizen of the United States. He was practically a piece of property and not a person. How long the black man has had to fight to secure his rights! There is, though, a more discriminated-against minority. The most helpless, the most pathetic, the most forgotten minority in America — or the world, for that matter — is the infant of the womb.

Thank God, the United States Supreme Court is not *the* Supreme Court. Supreme means highest. *The* Supreme Court is the bar of God's eternal justice, where many — oh, so many — of the verdicts of this world will be completely reversed!

In view of all this we should rise up in righteous anger against the horror of abortion. In our conversations we should speak against it. In our concern we should join the organizations that are marshaled against it. And, in the meanwhile, let the flag of our heart hang at half-mast for shame at this vilest stain on the pages of American law: the ongoing holocaust of the innocent unborn!

{ Cast Yourself Down! }

It was so startling a situation that our pedestrian minds, used to plodding the rut of routine, can hardly picture the scene. There was our Blessed Lord standing on the dizzying, pinnacled roof of the temple of Jerusalem, with Satan suavely coaxing Him to jump.

"If you are the Son of God, cast yourself down! You will not drop like a stone but float down gently like a feather. You will not crash among those people walking across the courtyard. Angels will bear you up. Prove to us that you are God's Son. Cast yourself down!"

And Jesus calmly answered that it was not right for anyone (not even the Messiah) anywhere (not even on the holy temple) to tempt the providence of God. In thus telling off the devil, was not our Savior also giving a gentle comeuppance to rash and presumptuous Christians? For example? The falsely optimistic ones who deliberately dare to put themselves in a serious occasion of sin, and then when they feel they must fall, cry out frantically to God, and expect Him to wave a magic wand and save them. Is not this also tempting the providence of God?

"Cast yourself down!" To the devil, a decent, practicing Catholic stands high up there on the pinnacle of the temple, because he lives by high moral standards, cherishes high ideals, and is, in brief, what we call a high type. He rises far above the low tide of corruption that may ooze and crawl around him. To him the devil often whispers, "Cast yourself down! Be like all those sensible people down there who spend their lives cutting corners. Why do you have to be so high and mighty about this religion bit? Drop down and join the crowd!"

True, Satan does not speak the same message vocally, but he certainly uses the world and the flesh to get it across. Anyone who has really tried to be loyal to the commandments of God, faithful to a Christian life, determined to follow in the footsteps of Christ, knows that this lofty program is anything but easy. The world all about us goes whistling and laughing along its smooth, broad boulevard of sin, while we are trying to climb the steep, narrow path of duty, climbing and stumbling and falling and picking ourselves up and starting all over again — and it can be such a lonely, uphill struggle!

And precisely because we are struggling to be good, because our goal is higher than the goals of the rest, we hear the soft, persuasive whisper: "Cast yourself down! Relax! Live modern! For one thing, enjoy Sunday and don't let religion get in the way. Half of America never goes to church anyway. . .

"Or, if you are weary of your marriage, turn in your present partner for a new, streamlined model. Divorce is just another up-to-date convenience for the home, like an automatic dishwasher. For the same reason, take advantage of artificial birth control. You don't have to burden yourself with children. The less family, the more chance for fun. . .

"Just come down from that ivory tower of yours. It is like the pinnacle of the temple, and you look so singular up there with your lofty code of conduct. Take the plunge. Let yourself go. Cast yourself down. My angels" — the devil whispers (though they are fallen angels) — "will bear you up! You will float down to a bed of roses. There will then be no commandments to cramp your style, no Church laws to interfere with your wishes, no confession to make you shine a flashlight upon the dark corners of your conscience.

"Life will be so much more comfortable without religion and without restraint. Cast yourself down! Forget Christ and follow the crowd!"

This is the advice you get from that unholy trinity: the devil, the world, and the flesh. And it is hard to refute, because it never has been easy to be a good Catholic. Our temptations may not come dramatically, as they did to Christ on the pinnacle of the temple, but come they do, and we wonder: When will they ever end? But it may help to remember that the agent of Satan who urges you, "Come down to earth, man!" is himself already in the mud.

On your job you may work in an office or a factory where sometimes the conversation around you comes from throats like sewers gurgling out filth and scum. You may work shoulder to shoulder with such people; but as God sees the scene, you are like a clean, snowy peak, rising above the crawling swamp. Don't come down!

It is the same way with a decent girl. She does not go in for drinking parties and does not allow liberties. And the world's reaction is, "Come down from your high horse! Why do you think you are so different?" And if she does come down, they look down on her. *Now* she is cheap, common, and rates about as high as yesterday's soiled newspaper. Now she is a flower that has already been plucked, a mountain that has already been scaled. She no longer stands like a quiet rebuke to their loose living. She has come down from the pinnacle of the temple. She is now just one of the crowd.

"Cast yourself down!" the devil whispers in your ear. But sometimes Satan fiddles his favorite tune in reverse, not "Cast yourself down!" but "Be downcast! Give up hope!" He knows that when the candle of our courage flickers low, when we feel as gloomy as a tombstone spattered with rain, when we are utterly despondent — he knows that this is his best opportunity. The devil loves to fish in troubled waters. In this sense, to be downcast or cast down might mean to be cast away — and with Saint Paul we must then *look up* to God, the God of all consolations.

We need the courage of a Columbus, who never turned back as his little ship plunged through dark and stormy waters, so that he could plant the cross of Christ on a new continent. The continent we have to conquer is our own self. On Columbus's ship, there were even some ex-criminals. We too have villainous urges aboard, and must put down the mutiny. In his crew were whiners and cowards. We too have nagging fears and sudden impulses that urge us to turn back and to give up. But, like Columbus, we must sail on!

If we are neither downcast through discouragement, nor heed the devil's plea to "Cast yourself down" by lowering our standards, we shall find that God's angels will bear us up higher than the pinnacle of the temple, even as high as the heights of heaven. How do we know? Christ was there before us!

c h a p t e r   f o u r

UNION OF THE SAINTS

{ Saint Joseph }

It is hard to imagine social friction in heaven; but during the month of March, Saint Patrick and Saint Francis Xavier must hurry past Saint Joseph with averted face and downcast eyes. They are embarrassed.

The month of March — at least in New England — is big for Saint Francis Xavier, especially with the famous novena of grace which used to pack churches from March 4 through March 12 and is now seeing a rebirth. Saint Patrick, of course, got the parties, the dances, and parades. Theoretically, to be sure, Saint Joseph got the whole month: at least it is dedicated to him in the liturgy of the laity that we all learned from the good nuns.

But how many Catholics who grope out of bed on the nineteenth of March are even vaguely aware that this day is the feast of Saint Joseph? Feast or not, to most Catholics it is only another drab day in the desert of Lent. In March Saint Francis gets the novenas, Saint Patrick gets the parades, and Saint Joseph gets the fast shuffle.

Even the traditional hymn that schoolchildren used to sing on Saint Joseph's feast day was enough to make any average twelve-year-old boy wince: "Dear Guardian of Mary, dear Nurse of her Child. . . ." What a sickening translation of the original Latin, *"Parvuli nutricie!"* — which means one who nurtures (that is, one who brings up, cares for, guards, protects).

And imagine the towering responsibility *that* was! Some years ago a collection of emeralds toured the museums of America. Called "The Crown of the Andes," it was far more precious than its weight in diamonds, a flashing dazzle of green brilliance that blinded the eye. The Pinkerton men assigned to guard it had some very anxious moments. When one of them mentioned this to a Secret Service man, the latter said, "You don't know worry! You should have been with us. When you were crossing the States, we were in Mexico with President Eisenhower, and every day he insisted on standing up and waving in an open car! Riding through those pushing crowds! It's a wonder our hair didn't turn gray!"

I wonder what Saint Joseph would have said to either of them. It was his job to guard the world's greatest treasures, the two most important figures in the history of the world, the Son of God and His Mother, Mary.

At least once in the discharge of that duty Joseph must have felt he failed so badly that it broke his heart. This, of course, was at Bethlehem, where the best he could come up with, seeking hearth and home for the newborn Child, was a forlorn stable. Under the Star, a stable — what could be more dismal! But it turned out that this was precisely what God wanted. It was the only way the Almighty could make an impression on the dull minds of men. It was the only way He could dramatize the birth of His Son.

Who can point out today where Julius Caesar was born? Who *can* say it was beneath the ruins of this elegant villa — or for that matter, who cares? But who can ever forget the little Babe stirring in the crackling straw of an animal's feedbox? Joseph could tell us that if you do your best, God will do the rest. Bethlehem seemed like the pathetic failure of Joseph, but it turned out to be the towering triumph of God.

Yet Joseph was not only the saint of the well-intentioned failure. He was also the saint of honest, humble labor. Besides guarding the Holy Family, Joseph also had to support them. This meant a job. This meant his hands were not just folded in prayer. They swung the pounding hammer and they pushed the groaning saw. Under his golden halo one could say that Joseph said his rosary in beads of salty sweat. Hard calluses quietly proclaimed that he was the patron of noble Christian work.

Yes, Christian work, because Joseph lived at a time when the pagan Greek and Roman aristrocrats looked down their patrician noses at physical labor. Such tasks were something assigned to the servants or shunted off to the slaves. Remember the phrase in the old catechism about servile work being forbidden on Sunday? This was in reference to the grunting labor done by slaves or the work carried out by servants. Looking back, we can see that the pagan empire was a huge gaudy pyramid resting on the bent backs of sweating slaves.

Christianity (of which Joseph was a forerunner) took a completely different view of work. Work atoned for original sin. Work fulfilled man's nature. Work was a sacrifice to the Almighty on the altar of man's physical human nature.

Like the pen of the writer or the brush of the artist, the tool of the craftsman lifted man above the beast. The difference between the man and the monkey would always be the monkey wrench. Of course Joseph did not need these philosophical distinctions. He had only to glance toward the Figure at the workbench beside him — a Figure whose only halo was a drift of golden sawdust — to realize that work was not something to be despised but something to be held in high honor. In his own way a craftsman was a king!

Joseph had the King of Kings for his helper. It makes

you wonder if some of the wisdom that later fell from the lips of Christ may not have been echoes of what Jesus had heard from Joseph.

For instance, Joseph was a carpenter in a country that had little wood. Most of the little cottages were built of stone. Still Jesus could easily have heard from Joseph, "If this be so in the greenwood, what will it be in the dry?" Or, "Build not your house on sand but on the solid rock." It comes down to what any master might say to an apprentice: "Never do a shoddy job!"

We call a workman's wages his salary, and everybody has heard that "salary" comes from the Latin word *sal* meaning salt. In early days salt was always part of the worker's pay. Hence the question, "Is he worth his salt?" It is still a pertinent question today. Does the workman give an honest day's work for an honest day's pay? Does he spend too much time on coffee break or at the water cooler or simply watching the clock? Does he call in sick when he is just sick of showing up for work?

Employers, of course, have their own obligations, like providing a just wage, furnishing decent working conditions, making available accident insurance, supplying pension benefits, and the like. But most of this is covered by law.

The worker, on the other hand, can soldier on the job (that is, loaf when no one is looking), cut corners — so much depends on the individual. Here steps in the memory of Joseph who in his work was as straight as his carpenter's square.

This is why Saint Joseph has a special and vivid appeal for the modern workingman. He is as far away as you can get from the traditional saint blazing in a stained-glass window. If ever a saint lived in a material, no-nonsense world, a world of hard wood and sharp nails, a world of noise and dust, a world of bruises and blisters, a world ten

63

thousand miles removed from the contemplative mystic —
that saint was Joseph. Yet still a mystic!

The point is, that even in that world of work Joseph
never forgot the nearness of God. When our Lord was only
a Baby, Joseph worked *for* Him. Later he worked *with*
Him, at the very side of Christ. For Joseph that place was
at a carpenter's bench. For us our place of work may be a
department-store counter, or a kitchen stove, or a
schoolroom chalkboard, or an office switchboard, or even
an operating table. Our glance toward Christ can be a brief
prayer, up and away that streaks off like a bird — a good
intention quickly made, a swift offering-up of what we are
doing. That momentary aspiration can turn even drab,
prosaic work into something bright and glorious just as a
setting sun, striking a row of dingy, grimy windows, can
turn these into squares of burnished gold.

So our routine work becomes a radiant prayer. And
with that prayer goes the comforting thought that after
life's labor will come eternal rest, in the hallowed company
of Jesus and Joseph, and that blessed bond between them,
our Lady herself!

} Saint Patrick {

About twelve centuries ago a hooded Irish monk blew on
his cold, cramped fingers and gratefully laid down his fine-
pointed quill, sighing, "Thanks be to God! It is finished!"
What he had finished was the Book of Kells, a gloriously
illuminated copy of the Holy Gospels. Each page glows
with the rainbow splendor of a tiny stained-glass window.
If the first letter on the page was an *S*, it became a spotted,
iridescent serpent. If it was a *T*, there was a crimson blood-
running cross. On every page the gold leaf still shimmers
like sunrise on a tropical sea. When the Book of Kells was
completed, the calendar read 800 or thereabouts.

But it was nearly four hundred years earlier that Patrick stood on a green wooded hill in Wicklow and watched the River Dardle go dashing down to the sea. The marvel is that the memory of Patrick, who lived centuries before the Book of Kells, is as bright and vivid as any of its pages today. Do you know of any other saint of the fifth century who is so widely known, so warmly loved, so enthusiastically remembered in this latter day when men have brushed moondust off their shoetops?

The day when Patrick stood on that Wicklow hill, he held in his hand a bishop's crosier. But, years before, his younger hands had gripped the gnarled staff of a swineherd. Then he stood in the midst of the grunting pigs, as a slave. In a dream an angel had appeared to him and bade him escape, and — miraculously — he did. Off to France then to study under his uncle, Saint Martin of Tours. Then to Rome and the holy pontiff Celestine. When Pope Celestine saw this monument of a man arise from the consecration ceremony with flowing cope and tall miter, he said, "They tell me your name in Gaelic is Succat. I change it now to Patricius, because you have the mold and bearing of a patrician, someone noble, aristocratic, regal."

The documents here may not be too dependable, but they say that Patrick was sixty years old when he set out to convert Ireland. Convert Ireland? It has the strange ring of someone setting out to baptize a cardinal! But this, of course, was in the dim twilight of long ago, when Ireland was pagan. Someone has smilingly divided Ireland's history into three eras: the pagan era, the Christian era, and De Valera.

Patrick plunged into Ireland with the fierce zeal of an anointed prophet. On the hill of Slane he dared to burn the carved wooden idols of the Druids and light the famous Easter fire, which was like lighting the sanctuary lamps that would burn in Irish sanctuaries forever.

It turned out to be a lovely land, an emerald isle set in a silver sea. Walk a leisurely mile and you can see a dozen different shades of green sparkling with the diamonds of the morning dew. Its hills wear the morning mist like a fine gray shawl. Its lakes are so softly blue they could be melted sky. Its whitewashed cottages are bright with red rambler roses that blaze like a stand of vigil lights.

Patrick found its people pagan only in their ignorance of the Gospel. In character they had a natural nobility that became a deep loyalty to their new faith. That is why Ireland never spawned a heresy. That is why it was willing to make monumental sacrifices for the faith. How it suffered through the centuries! Is it an accident that the shamrock is a tiny green Celtic cross? For three hundred years Ireland hung upon the tortured cross of religious persecution. For three hundred years its history was written with a thorn dipped in blood. How ironic that Ireland's most glorious oratory was not spoken from holy pulpits or historic platforms but from the prisoner's dock in grim courtrooms by men who would next stand on the trapdoor of a gibbet. These were the long, bloody days when Ireland's wayside shrines were the stark silhouettes of gallows, and when the halos of its heroes were yellow hemp loops.

Who can count the price Ireland paid for keeping the Catholic faith? It is easy to go to Mass when you are answering the call of chiming church bells and serenely make your way to an impressive edifice with hundreds of your neighbors. But who will say it is easy to steal out in the cold dawn to a lonely, secret spot in the hills, and gather with other "outlaws" around the Mass Rock where the tinkle of the altar bell might be drowned by the baying of the king's bloodhounds and the crackle of the king's rifles?

In those grim times the price on a priest's head, payable to any informer, was thirty pounds. Does it not bring up sour memories of Judas, an earlier informer, and thirty pieces of silver?

It is easy to be a Catholic if before the law you are as good as the next man, having all your rights, and standing tall within them. But it is another thing if you have been stripped of your rights: if, for example, you as a Catholic are not allowed admission to college, if you cannot belong to any profession, if you cannot even hold property. To be willing to sacrifice all this for the faith is saying "I believe!" — not with your lips but with your life.

The Catholic faith has had an enormous impact wherever the "wild geese" of Ireland have winged their way from their native shore. When you think of it, this impact is out of all proportion to the size of the little place they left. Ireland is only a tiny green island in a swirling gray sea, so sparsely populated that there are only a little more than a hundred people to the square mile. It is barren of significant resources. Its bogs do not bubble rich black oil. Its hills are not veined with coal or streaked with gold. Its landscape is not crowned with rich forests. Its harbors are not bustling with ships sending exports to all parts of the globe.

What Ireland produces cannot be packed into crates or poured into barrels. It was essentially the spirit that Patrick bequeathed, the deep faith and the warm heart, the witty tongue and the lilting song, and a fierce dedication to freedom. It is Ireland's contribution to the brave and multicolored mosaic of that grand Catholic image produced by so many different nationalities that together have made the Church in America the magnificent enterprise it is.

They say that every institution is the lengthened shadow of a man. Ireland is not the shadow of Saint Patrick. It is the bright sun behind him.

{ Saint Alphonsus }

Till this warm June day the middle-aged Redemptorist priest has stridden through life in vigorous, ruddy health. Now suddenly he finds himself lying in his simple iron bedstead, teetering on the dark brink of death. Through this long day he moves in and out of consciousness like a train passing in and out of dim tunnels. A doctor holds the feeble, fluttering pulse and frowns. A priest comes forward with the holy oils and presses a warm, anointing thumb on eyes and ears and hands of the limp figure. The dying man's father, a grizzled Navy captain, stands by clenching and unclenching nervous fists. Everyone is waiting for the last mortal sigh.

Then all at once the man in the bed opens his eyes. He stretches out trembling hands. "Give me," he says, "my little statue of the Madonna!" They think he must be murmuring some delirious nonsense, so they pay no attention. But this time he says it again, louder and clearer: "Bring me my little Madonna!" Someone goes over to the simple bureau and takes the small colored statue and places it in the dying man's moist fingers. He reaches out, clasps it, kisses it, holds it before him with shining eyes.

All at once it happens. Even as they strain forward to see, out of that lifeless little image of Mary, new life pours into the wan figure in the bed. From weak pallor he is transformed into pink, glowing health. Everyone in the room is startled at the sudden change, but someone whispers, "It is only a passing rally." The sick man hears it and shakes his head. "No," he insists, "I am cured. I am well again." And he certainly was.

A passing rally? As a matter of record, he outlived every person in that room. If this had been a passing rally, it went on till the patient passed ninety. So grateful was

Alphonsus to our Lady for that miraculous recovery that for the rest of his long life he signed his name as Alphonsus Mary de Liguori. Later, when he founded the Redemptorist Order, he hung our Lady's fifteen-decade rosary on his cassock in place of the elegant dress sword that he had worn as a Neapolitan noble and had hung up at her shrine. The jingle of the sword was gone, but the soft rattle of the beads kept her memory clicking at his side.

Once Padre Alfonso was back on his feet again, he plunged once more into his former energetic, dedicated life. One week you might find him on the docks at Naples preaching to the beggars (the lazzaroni) who squatted the hours away, soaking up the sun. The following week Alphonsus would be high in the green hills beyond Naples, holding up his crucifix and explaining the Gospel to the goatherds in those remote mountains.

These people loved him, not for his message alone but for the compassionate way he delivered it. This was a time in the Church when grim religious severity and iron strictness held sway. Alphonsus, on the contrary, held high the banner of sweet and gentle mercy.

Just about this time Alphonsus was designated as the archbishop of Palermo but somehow managed to elude that honor. However, eventually Rome overruled his humble protests and set the miter on his graying hair as the bishop of a smaller diocese called Saint Agatha of the Goths. The previous bishop had left behind a gorgeous pectoral cross and a thick gold ring with large precious stones. The day after Alphonsus took over the see of Saint Agatha of the Goths, he sold the cross and ring and bought himself a cheap gilt cross and a simple brass ring and gave the difference to the poor. He said, "How could I go about sparkling with gold and gems when my people are struggling to survive?"

Looking back now, through the rearview mirror of

history, we can see how the influence of Alphonsus went out far beyond his little diocese. Somehow, it brings to mind the plaque that hangs in the magnificent church of Saint Paul's in London. Here you see impressive monuments and glittering marble tombs, but you look in vain for any statue of the man responsible for all this architectural glory. But then you come upon a simple bronze plaque and the inscription that reads: "Sir Christopher Wren. If you seek his monument, just look around."

If you look around — not in Saint Paul's but in the average Catholic church — you will find a silent monument to Saint Alphonsus. Look at the Tabernacle, and you remember that he wrote that precious booklet *Visits to the Blessed Sacrament for Every Day of the Month*, worldwide in its circulation. Look at the Stations of the Cross, and remember that his *Way of the Cross* was the standard text for generations of Catholics in Lent. Look at our Lady's shrine and recall that his book *The Glories of Mary* has been translated more than any other volume on Mary. Look at the confessionals and realize that by Roman decree Alphonsus is the patron of confessors.

Almost a hundred years ago Canon Sheehan, the famous Irish writer, said that if a missionary were to leave tomorrow for some distant heathen shore, he would have to take with him, light though his luggage must be, four indispensable books: Bible, Missal, Breviary, and the moral theology of Saint Alphonsus Liguori.

There have been other manuals to guide confessors, but too often they were written by well-meaning men who were high-domed theorists, separated from the actual world by tall bookcases. Such writings tend to be so far removed from reality, so utterly impractical, that they make the active confessor wince and groan.

Saint Alphonsus was never one of these. No mouse of the scrolls he, but a man who had spent forty years slogging along the muddy roads of mission life, going from parish to parish, preaching and hearing confessions. The result was that when he sat down to write his book on moral theology, his viewpoint was not from a remote, academic library ladder but from practical day-to-day experience in the trenches. He knew human nature not from reading books but from endless hours behind a confessional screen.

Not that he thought he knew it all. He never poached on the pope's domain of infallibility. Every year he learned, and — what is more significant — unlearned. His tomes on moral theology are massive volumes, and since this is not an exact science but rather a system of informed, prudent opinions, there was plenty of room to be wrong. Would you believe that this man had the humility to make ninety-nine corrections in the second edition of his great work? A saint cares nothing for personal vanity. He seeks only the truth, or as close to it as he can come.

No wonder that popes in chorus have praised Alphonsus. Pius IX hailed him as the saint who beat down the pessimistic heresy of Jansenism. Leo XIII held him up as the most distinguished yet the mildest of moralists. Pius XII said that though Alphonsus lived two hundred years ago, "He is a theological giant who belongs to our age." Is it any wonder that eight hundred bishops petitioned the Holy See to elevate him to that high and heady honor, Doctor of the Church? (In this sense, doctor refers to doctrine, an accredited teacher of the truth.)

Saint Alphonsus baffled the actuaries of his day, when life expectancy was pegged at about fifty, by passing ninety. Two days before he died, a Redemptorist brother was pushing Alphonsus in his wheelchair down the monastery corridor in the tiny Italian town of Nocera. This was the last time the saint was to leave his room. As they creaked along the corridor, bishop and brother had always said the beads together, but now the old man's head was so stooped into his chest with arthritis and his voice so feeble that the brother could hardly hear the Hail Marys.

The next day Alphonsus could not make it into the wheelchair for his cherished rosary ride. Instead he said: "Please prop me up and read me something about our Lady." After listening awhile he said, "I like that. Who wrote it?" The brother said, "Why, you did!" Saints do not bluff, and Alphonsus was not bluffing. When you have written a hundred books and pamphlets, how can you recognize a page from one of them?

The next day he was too weak even to listen to any reading. Instead he stretched out his hand and whispered, "Give me my little Madonna!" So they put into his shaky hand the small picture of our Lady (like the little statue of years ago) which always stood on his desk. Around his bed the priests and brothers began to intone the Litany of the Saints, but before they had reached the end, he had taken his place among the halos they were invoking.

Who can doubt that Alphonsus was at that moment warmly received by the Queen of Saints? Long before the doctrine of Mary's Immaculate Conception was officially proclaimed, he had written in its defense. Alphonsus championed our Lady's high status with the precision of a theologian, but he loved her with the warmth of the Italian sun. His feast day is August 1. Hers is August 15. Close on the calendar, they must be even closer in heaven: Mary and Alphonsus Mary, Mother and son.

{ **Blessed Peter Donders** }

It was Oliver Wendell Holmes who said, "No man is an entomologist. There are too many bugs." In somewhat the same way you might say that no man is a hagiographer;

not that there are too many saints but that they are so different. They follow no pattern. They come from molds as varied as that which produced the gentle Little Flower of Jesus and the testy and crochety Saint Jerome.

Some saints are household names. Some are unknown. Unknown — that is, like the Unknown Soldier — except to God, who knows them quite well. Place in this latter group Blessed Peter Donders, who is a modern saint, beatified as late as 1983. Granted that technically he is not yet a saint, but as one beatified he is waiting in the vestibule and should be summoned any time now and handed a highly deserved halo. He has his feast day already, January 14.

Born in Holland near the beginning of the last century, young Peter was drawn from early youth toward the priesthood. But his family was as poor as Nazareth, so college and seminary seemed as remote as heaven. Far from expecting financial help from his parents, he had to get a job in a factory to help support younger brothers and sisters. After a spell he managed to obtain a position as a kind of general servant and all-around handyman in a Dutch college. At least now he lived near books and in the world of the mind.

Never undersell divine providence! An affluent supervisor there was quietly watching this young Donders, noting that he was conscientious in his duties and quite the gentleman in his manners. Suddenly out of the blue came the green, or at least the Dutch banknotes, from this offstage patron to pay for tuition at college and seminary. The day would come when Peter Donders would be credited with miracles attributed to his intercession; but this time he was on the grateful receiving end, surprised and delighted.

Toward the end of his seminary course, young Donders happened to pick up a magazine whose pages glowed with the romance and the adventure of foreign missions. These were the pictures. If you read the text, you learned of the hardships and the sacrifices. Together they appealed vividly to the youth and the zeal of Peter Donders. This, he thought, is for me: danger, risk, faraway places, strange people, a modern apostle!

At that time, it seems that Holland had priests like tulips or windmills, and the local bishop frowned on oversaturation. He told young Donders that he would ordain him if he promised to leave his country and serve as a foreign missionary. Peter must have smiled because this was precisely what he yearned for and dreamed about. He was being commanded to do just what he secretly wanted: to go to a foreign mission.

The mission territory in question turned out to be Dutch Guiana, now the republic of Surinam, on the northern coast of South America. It is a curious statistic that it took the young priest forty-six days (days of calm and storm and swinging rhythmic seas) to reach his destined port. He stayed there until he died forty-five years later, without ever coming home. Saints are different.

They assigned him first to Paramaribo, a thriving town by the standards of that day and place. At least there were houses and stores and roads. To the natives it was Camelot. Here the Dutch planters aspired to create a new little Holland on the equator, an urbane pocket of colonial prosperity with elegant homes and country-club luxury.

But Father Donders had not come this far to live as if he had never left home at all. Soon afterward he found that the working plantations were six hours away by boat on the narrow rivers that reached like long brown fingers into the jungle. Here poor blacks, taken from Africa, toiled in the tropical sun, their bodies streaming with sweat. It was slavery pure and simple, or at least simple. Here the young priest went, week after week, now to this plantation, now to that, preaching the Gospel and offering the comfort of his compassionate heart. The slaves loved him; the planters hated him but somehow did not stop him. Beneath the surface the conscience of Holland winced. Quietly but firmly the young priest began to call attention to this outrage and pleaded for the freedom of the slaves.

In the jungle the insect life, crawling and buzzing, tortured him. The strange food sickened him. Danger was never far from him. Once a mad slave, thinking that the white priest was a hated planter, seized him by the throat and had him half-strangled when other slaves dragged the deranged man off. How happy Father Donders must have felt years later when the fight for freedom of the blacks that he had championed suddenly erupted into glorious success! By a sweet coincidence, it was in 1863, the very year when the slaves were emancipated in the United States.

While at the town of Paramaribo, Donders heard of a place to the west called Batavia. It was not far from Devil's Island. That was bad enough, but near Batavia was a sinister spot that nature itself had isolated from the surrounding countryside. High hills rimmed it round like the green sides of a great bowl. Brown roads ran past it as if afraid to come near. No wonder! Who wants to drop in on a leper colony? Six hundred poor victims lived there, abandoned and forgotten.

At first Father Donders just visited them. Then he got permission to live among them. He did this while thirty Christmases, none of them white, passed over his graying head. He would meet the new patients that the ship brought in, and do his best to comfort them in their first trying lonely days. That was the worst time, the early heartbreaking hours when they realized that they were like people living on another planet, exiles excluded from the world itself.

In our time the word leprosy is frowned upon. It is now Hansen's disease, but, like the rose called by any other name, the horror is still there. Many of those at Batavia were frightful to look upon, but they were Peter Donders's parish, the family to which he was "Father." He looked at their blighted faces as he read the Gospel of the Mass, led their quavering voices in the old familiar hymns, reminded them in his sermons that the gentle Christ had never spurned a leper.

Priest he was; paramedic he had to be, wrapping bandages around their ulcerous sores. No task was too humble. He split the wood and fetched armfuls for their fires, carried pails of water from the wells, often cooked their food, and at the end dug their graves. But looming above all he did was the shining presence of what he was. They could never forget the towering truth that when all the world seemed to forget them, here was a man, a messenger of the crucified Christ, who cared.

This was one of the prime problems, their grim conviction that out there practically nobody did care. Sullen anger burned deep within them like a vein of coal smoldering deep beneath the ground. A furious feeling of helplessness and hopelessness would roll across the colony like a rising wave and then break off into whimpering despair. Was anybody out there concerned? Did anybody even know?

Enter here the practical and, if you will, even the political, Father Donders. He knew that alone he could do little. But he remembered how he had successfully lobbied for the freedom of the black slaves on the plantation, so now he raised high the banner and sounded the trumpet for these ignored lepers. And he kept at it. To the government he was probably like a pesty, persistent fly, buzzing and biting all the time and never at rest. But it had its effect. Doctors and medical teams were dispatched to the colony. At last, someone cared enough about the plight of these people — suffering and dying, and in effect left by the side of the road — to do something about it.

After a grinding day, when darkness dropped over the colony huts, Father Donders would make his way to the church, and hour after hour pace back and forth saying his endless prayers. They say that the very boards of the floor were worn with his footsteps. When he was asked why he said his prayers walking, he smiled and said, "I have two reasons. One, so I don't fall asleep. And two, I am then only a moving target for the mosquitoes." They say he never slapped a mosquito. The saints *are* different.

The years passed and the Redemptorists were given charge of the Batavia territory, including the leper colony. These Redemptorists were from Holland, so Father Donders asked to join their order. After the requisite novitiate he was accepted. But irony upon irony! Now he was fifty-seven; long ago, when he was only twenty-seven, he had applied to the Redemptorists and been turned away with smooth velvet regrets. To the obvious taunt that we Redemptorists cannot tell a saint when we see one, we subjoin this consoling fact: the Jesuits and the Franciscans had waved him away too.

At this time the Redemptorists sent another priest to assist Father Donders, and this allowed him to do something he had wanted to do for some time. Deep in the neighboring jungle lived the Carib Indians, spiritual orphans if ever there were. Father Donders initiated a program to visit them every few months. They were a dull, slow, lethargic tribe, and Father Donders used to come back shaking his saintly head and admitting that he had to repeat the Our Father hundreds of times.

But Peter Donders was now in his seventies, and his religious superiors decided he should be relieved of the taxing work at the leper colony. He, of course, did not want to go. The lepers were heartbroken to see him go. He told them simply, "I must go. I must obey. But I have a feeling I shall return and I shall die among you."

Two years later the priest at the leper colony took sick, and Father Donders was sent back to replace him, at least for the time. No sooner there, Father Donders became ill. When the doctor asked, "How do you feel?" he answered with the smiling evasion of a saint, "I have nothing to complain about." Then when the doctor had left, he turned to those in the little hut. "This is Wednesday, isn't is? I'll die on Friday about three in the afternoon."

And he did. Having followed Christ in life, he followed His pattern in death. What a grand reunion there must have been between him and that other Apostle of the Lepers, Father Damien! Down here almost everyone has heard of Father Damien. Practically nobody has heard of Father Donders. Does it greatly matter?

chapter five

HUMAN QUIRKS

{ The Smaller World }

Snap open your crisp newspaper any morning and the headlines hit you, big and black, like the top line of an optician's chart. Big type for big doings, the great events of yesterday: treaties or strikes or battles, a train wreck or a plane crash, perhaps a medal presented at a banquet, maybe a man murdered in a bank. The high drama and the shrill tone of the front page.

But there are other pages. A newspaper is not all streaming and screaming headlines. The lesser happenings are tucked away in tiny type inside. And these are the things, the small paragraphs, that touch so much more closely the lives of most people.

All around us may whirl the clash and clatter of great events — the test of a nuclear bomb, a voyage to the moon, a Supreme Court decision, a scientific expedition — but we never get closer to them than the television screen. They happen, of course, but they do not touch us personally. We read of great achievements, but we live in a little world of our own. We live our little private lives with other little people. We live on a little globe whose little continents are no farther away than our home, our office, our school, our church, our friends.

It is not a world of statesmen and astronauts and scientists. It is a personal world of smiles and frowns and snubs and compliments and hidden worries and sudden joys and unexpected heartaches, a parade of minor emergencies and small crises. The other big world is outside our windows, remote.

We read the headline: UNITED NATIONS WEIGHS CENSURE. Everybody reads it with a kind of dull, distant interest, but who really cares? Despite everything, you turn the page and see a tiny item about a ten-year-old boy who while riding his bike is hit by a car and how it is feared he has a fractured skull. Behind those lines is a home where the bike used to stand in the cellar or garage and where there are tears and low voices and tense, terrible hours of waiting. This is the kind of news that touches people's lives. This is our world.

Compared to a plunge in the stock market or the capture of a skyjacker, a boy on a bike may not be startling news; but a happening is important or unimportant only as it affects us. We can't do much to change the big world around us, but we can do something to make our own little world better (the world of the people with whom we live or work or chum) and make life as happy and decent for them as we can.

Here, like the tiny paragraphs of small news, it is the little things that count, that make the difference. After all, what is life but a jigsaw puzzle of little pieces we try to fit in together as smoothly as we can? It reminds one of the gray-haired husband who said with a twinkle in his eye that when he married, he and his wife made an agreement: She was to decide all the little things and he would make the decision in all the big, important matters. "Looking back," he mused, "our life must have been a very simple one, because in the forty years of our married life I never had to make a decision."

Sometimes little incidents can develop into sad situations, just as a small ulcerated tooth can send poison crawling through the whole system. In the same fashion, one deliberate slight can poison a long friendship. Curious how we call it a slight, but to the receiver it never seems slight. It is monumental and monstrous. We talk of sleight of hand that makes a coin or card disappear; but slight of tongue in the social sense can make a friend disappear, and there is no magician who can bring him or her back again.

Sometimes the impulse to say something sharp and hurting is almost irresistible. Sometimes it is harder to hold back a crushing retort than to hold back wild horses. Sometimes the hardest thing in the world to make is not an atom bomb but an allowance, an allowance for someone who has hurt us deeply. Sometimes it is harder to bury a grievance than it is to bury a beloved relative. But if we do not say harsh things ourselves, and if we overlook them when said to us, we are taking Christianity off the shelf and bringing it down into our daily lives.

But that is only half the platform of Christ: not just avoiding the nasty little things that hurt but also doing the bright little things that help our neighbors. We all can strike our breasts and admit that through indifference or laziness or sheer selfishness we don't do half the kind acts we could. Like the rips in a fisherman's net which let his silver catch slither out, these thin, weak areas in our character let many golden chances for doing some little good deed slip away.

For example, would it have been so hard to get out the note paper and envelope and stamp, and send that letter of sympathy when Helen's father or Jim's mother died? It caused them many tears; couldn't we spare a few drops of ink?

Or would it have torn a terrible hole in our week to spend an evening with Aunt Mary in the hospital? Oh, she had get-well cards on the bureau, and flowers in the window, and candy on the little stand; but during her lonely hours she must have longed for a well-known face in the doorway, a smile from someone who really cared.

And how about the time you had the inspiration to bring so-and-so to confession? You knew he had been away for a long time. You felt that with a little tact and gentle playing on the line you could land him, because he really wanted to come back. You knew (and he knew) that he would take the first hard step — into the confessional — with reluctance; but he would leave it with relief, and with the wonderful feeling that he was walking on air, tiptoeing along the high white clouds of God's forgiveness. But somehow you never brought the matter up, and to this day he has never had the courage to lay his burden down. You — well, you forgot. "Forgot." There is the epitaph of so many good deeds that died undone, the stillborn babes of Christian kindness who never saw the light of day.

Once a well-dressed man stopped a ragged youngster as he was running into the tenement where he lived. "Tell me, son," he said, "do you really believe that God is good?" "Why, sure!" said the boy. "But if He is so good," persisted the man, "why doesn't He tell somebody to send you new clothes and other good things?" The lad had never thought of this before, so he shrugged his shoulders and said very earnestly, "I guess He does tell somebody, but somebody always forgets."

This may sound like a heart-and-flowers appeal to religion, but actually it is only the Sermon on the Mount brought down to the sidewalk and the subway and to everyday life. God does not really *need* us to do good, but He *wants* to use us.

It is like that other boy in the Gospel, when there were thousands of hungry people dotting the hillside. "How much food have you?" Jesus asked the Apostles. They told Him there was a lad in the crowd with a basket of five loaves and a couple of fish. I don't know whether our Lord smiled. I know He did not sneer. He did not wave the youngster away and say, "Utterly inadequate! *I'll* take care of this." No, He took the boy's bread and fish and — after multiplying it — used it to feed the multitude.

It is the same today. All our Lord wants is that we place at His service not our basket of loaves and fish but our basket of love, of good will, of cooperation; and this, plus His power, can work wonders of which we do not dream!

So, in His name let us go forth and do little acts of kindness, not because it is a mark of culture (and not because it will win friends and influence people and be good for business), but because we do it in the name of God, the God who made man in His image, who lives behind "the million masks of man," whose divine Son is our Brother! When grace nudges our elbow and whispers in our ear to do some special little act of Christ-like kindness, may His Mother — and Our Mother of Perpetual Help — help us to hear and to heed and to do!

⎰ No More Church for Me! ⎱

People stop going to church for many reasons. Some just grow indifferent and stop gradually, like the propeller of a plane slowly flipping over till it comes to a dead halt because the engine has been turned off. The solution to that situation is simple: switch the engine on again. To put it another way, the honest man looks into the mirror of his conscience and finds no sounder grounds for giving up God than laziness or inconvenience. He skips church not because he does not need it but because it requires an effort.

There is another type of man that does not merely passively stay away from church but deliberately boycotts it because somewhere along the line he had a quarrel with a priest. (You would not believe it, of course, but some people do not like even me.) But refusing to darken the door of a church because of some incident with an individual clergyman is about as logical as never eating ice cream because you were once snubbed by an ice-cream vendor.

The third group is more pitiful still. They are not lazy, and they are not bitter; but they are sensitive and timid and tend to have tissue-paper souls. Deep inside they want to come to church often, to draw closer to God; but they stay away because they fear ridicule. To be honest, they do not merely fear it; they have felt it. Over the rattle of typewriters in the office, or against the clatter and tinkle of cash registers in the department store, or between shuffles at the bridge game — there are many places where you can hear the smart sarcastic remarks that the world reserves for those it considers too religious. By too religious is meant anyone who is foolish enough to drop into church during the week, or anyone who lets the hearts-and-flowers world of religion clash and interfere with the bread-and-butter world of reality.

As long as you limit your religious program to being only a fashionable and musical way of spending Sunday morning (on those Sundays when you have no other engagement), the modern world is understandingly tolerant. But once you go over that quota, once you let the spirit of religion seep into your daily life, once you let the ideals of Christ and Christianity run like a golden thread through the ordinary homespun fabric of routine everyday affairs, once you let your standards stand up against an inflated insurance claim or an expanded expense account or a crooked deal in business or a scurrilous attack on the Church or an appealing piece of political graft — then prepare to be ridiculed. The snipers will get you, and their shots can really hurt.

It is quite possible that there actually are men and women who, had they lived in the grim days of gory persecution, might have suffered gallantly for their faith; but in this soft and sneering time, when the persecution is ridicule, they wince and surrender. The one thing they cannot stand is ridicule. But today that may be the precise test: not being killed for your faith but being kidded. Not being surrounded by crackling flames but by cackling laughter. Not being tossed on the horns of a wild bull but being lifted ever so gently on a raised eyebrow. Is it possible that people have actually been taunted and laughed out of heaven and into hell?

Certainly the world has often tried it. Certainly the world has often tried to cram the dunce cap of the fool on the saints who wore an invisible golden halo. As a matter of fact, even beyond considerations of religion, almost everything on this old globe that ever grew into something worthwhile has been at some time or other fertilized with ridicule. Read the story of almost every great man and you find that the first notes of his trumpet of triumph were the braying laugh of some jackass. Did they not brand the first steamboat "Fulton's Folly"? Did they not mock the Suffragettes who only asked for what now everybody takes for granted — the right of women to go to the ballot box and vote?

In the area of religion, there were probably those who winked and smirked when Washington knelt in the snow at Valley Forge. Surely there were those who hooted Saint Francis out of his hometown of Assisi. Of course, the ordinary man does not think of himself against a dramatic background. He knows he is not a heroic figure, the photograph in the frontispiece of a book. He only knows that it is bitter medicine to be whispered about and laughed at because he practices, really practices and stands up for his faith.

He knows that it is not easy at work when other men insist on telling him dirty stories and he shows it is about as welcome as if they unloaded a garbage truck on his front lawn or in his living room. He knows that when he resents it and objects to it, he is put down as a mama's boy. He only knows that if he goes to a party where the girls arrive painted and then get plastered and the whole atmosphere is pagan and he shows he is uncomfortable they will want to know if his halo is on straight or if his wings are not sticking out. That sort of thing is very easy to ladle out but very hard to swallow.

And do you know why they ladle it out? Because deep down under the flamboyant jacket or the shimmering dress they are uneasy about their own conduct and more than a mite jealous of his. They know it takes courage to stand alone and be true blue, while anyone can be yellow and merely follow the crowd. They know that deep down in their own soul, their conscience is swinging and ringing like a lighthouse bell; but they do not want to hear it or heed it, so they try to keep talking louder and faster and (they hope) funnier. But secretly they are no heroes to themselves, not by a thousand miles, these loudmouths who scoff at the piety and the purity of others.

There is one other group we should mention, if we are to touch all the bases, and recognize even the splinter factions that have stopped going to church. This is the element whose members break out the flag of righteous anger and maintain they do not go to church because of all the hypocrites who do. They will tell you (if you are willing to listen) about Mr. Bourbon who gets stoned every Saturday night but who is still so loyal to the Rock of Peter that he will still go to Mass every Sunday morning or, nowadays, every Sunday afternoon. In fact he just about makes that. Or they will tell you about Mr. Ballot, the politician, who has one well-manicured hand in the holy water font and the other in the public till. Or they will tell you about Mrs. Tongue who goes to Mass every single morning but at the same time does a mass-production job in scandal. She gets her gossip wholesale and merchandises it retail. She has a tongue like an acetylene torch that manages to cut friendships in half with her vicious stories, but the same tongue is tilted toward heaven as she piously says her daily prayers.

This makes the people who have stopped going to church ask triumphantly: "Do you call this religion?" We, of course, who go to church are supposed to be flabbergasted, humiliated, and stopped. Well, the obvious answer is, "No, of course, we do not consider this religion." And what is more important — Almighty God surely does not consider it religion. But do these people really believe that this same Almighty God is going to accept that sad fact (that hypocrites also go to church) as a valid reason why other people should not go? On Judgment Day, God is not going to ask us to pass judgment on the deeds or misdeeds of others. When we are in the dock, the spotlight will entirely be upon us. That is why it is good to remember that in the restaurant of this life we pick up the check only for ourselves.

May the good Lord, then, be merciful to those high and mighty ones who in their majesty have decided not to go to church because people whom they consider hypocrites do. Two wrongs do not make a right. Weakness in others gets us no medals for being strong. For any such prodigal son and daughter we pray the gentle Mother of God to open their eyes, and take their hands, and lead them back to a God who is so good that He is willing to forgive even the folly of such as these!

chapter six

INSIDE THE CHURCH

{ Choosing a Bishop }

Though they have rarely pretended to reveal who voted for whom, the news media cover no story more completely than the election of a pope. From the moment that the red-robed cardinals enter their solemn conclave, some sweeping past in tall majesty and others shuffling along with the slouch and stoop of creeping years, the eyes and ears of the reporting world — radio and television and newspapers and magazines — are fixed on every step of the procedure. There are pictures of the cardinals' desks, facsimiles of the (blank) secret ballots, even glimpses into the kitchen where the food is prepared as for a sequestered jury. Not until that dramatic wisp of white smoke signals that one of the cardinals is doffing his flaming crimson and putting on the awful responsibilities of papal white, do the newsmen pack their gear and head for the next headline. Even at that they come back for the coronation.

In view of this worldwide exposure of the making of a pope, it is curious that Catholics on the whole know so little about the method by which a bishop, and specifically the bishop of their own diocese, is chosen. After all, the pope is remote, but the bishop is right in their midst. Should not the crew of a cruiser be at least as interested in the selection of its own captain as in the appointment of the distant admiral of the fleet? Do we never in our local diocesan minds wonder why it was that Monsignor Smith or (though this is a bit unusual) Father Jones should suddenly be elevated to the bishopric? Who decides that the scarlet skullcap should ceremoniously appear on the iron-gray hair of this priest or on the more slippery pate of the man in the next parish? Who actually does the selecting, and what are the qualifications that influence it?

If the precise answers to such questions, complete with all the fascinating details, could be given — page by page and chapter by chapter — it would make a book that would beat the Breviary as a best-seller among the clergy. In any event, the Iron Curtain or the Berlin Wall are frail summer screens compared to the secrecy that duly and justly surrounds the deliberations, the conversations, and the correspondence that precede the nomination of a bishop. The man who will henceforth be addressed as "Your Excellency," and who will prefix all future signatures with a jabbed sign of the cross, is not decided upon in Macy's window or in any ecclesiastical goldfish bowl.

Yet there is no secret at all about the process by which such a man is first rated as *episcopabilis* (that is, worthy of the bishopric), and it is from those so designated that the hierarchy are usually chosen. Apropos of this it is curious that the very first bishop not selected by our Savior Himself was chosen by lot, but even he still had to meet certain requirements. This replacement of the defecting Judas is vividly described in the first chapter of the Acts of the Apostles.

Listen to Peter as he addresses the one hundred and twenty brethren: "There are men among us who have walked in our company all through the time our Lord Jesus came and went among us, from the time when John used to baptize to the time Jesus was taken from us. One of these ought to be added to our number as a witness of His Resurrection." So they nominated two: Justus and Matthias — and prayed that God would show them the right man. Did the candidates then draw straws? Scripture simply says: "They cast lots; and the lot fell upon Matthias; and he took rank with the eleven Apostles."

In the early days of the Church, bishops were often elected by the priests, and sometimes by the people of the place. In small areas this was probably as effective a way as any to set the miter on the brow of the best equipped. When Saint Gregory the Wonder-worker was dying, he asked, "How many pagans are there still in my diocese?" They told him, "Seventeen." "Good," he smiled. "When I became bishop here, there were just seventeen Christians." In so small a diocese (how big was Neocaesarea in the middle of the third century?) priests and people could intelligently choose a prelate's capable and zealous successor. But in a huge twentieth-century American diocese, such voting could easily split the Catholic community into bitter factions or innumerable fragments. The whole thing would probably be chaotic, inevitably political, and of course is contrary to the present canon law.

But if a priest does not become a bishop through a popularity contest, or by ecclesiastical civil service with examinations and grades, or as a reward for seniority of service in the sanctuary, what is the process that does slide a bishop's ring on his finger and put the crosier into his hand? This is no dark secret at all. It is contained in a public document that anyone can read and that was first promulgated for the United States in 1916. Granted that it does not and cannot reveal the immediate reason why this or that particular priest makes the leap from the black to the purple, it does at least lift the lid from how the pool of candidates is assembled.

It must first be remembered that in the structure of the Church several adjacent dioceses form what is known as a province. For example, the Boston province is made up of the dioceses of Worcester, Springfield, Fall River, Manchester, Burlington, Portland, and the archdiocese of Boston. Every year each of these dioceses' bishops gets in touch with those older priests who are his diocesan consultors and asks them to submit in strictest confidence the names of those priests they deem worthy of becoming bishops. This might involve consulting, in person or by mail, about a dozen men. It is only fair to add that although the bishop is obliged to consult these men, he is not obliged to follow their counsel. How could he follow what might be twelve different suggestions?

To the list sent in, the bishop now adds his own choices, and then ponders and prays. After all this he selects two names and sends them to the archbishop of the province. He may, if he so wishes, send in two names that he has already nominated on previous occasions. Now questionnaires go out (again under ironclad secrecy) to several priests in each diocese, each of whom is presumed to have firsthand knowledge of the man he is queried about.

Incidentally, no bishop may propose a man for a miter unless that man is known to him personally. The questionnaires sent out to the priests in the field ask blunt questions like, "What is the state of the candidate's apparent health? Does he show zeal in his work? What about his learning? His piety? His record of administration? His temperament? His qualities of leadership?" And so on. It is as if the army were investigating an officer before giving him top-secret clearance.

When the questionnaires have been returned to the archbishop, the latter calls a quiet, informal meeting of the bishops soon after Easter. If possible, nobody is to know where they are gathering or why. This is God's business and no one else's. To emphasize God's place, the meeting is opened with a solemn oath taken on the Gospels, each bishop in turn laying his hand on the holy page and swearing never to reveal what is said at the meeting.

The theory is that in such a vacuum of secrecy no one need ever hesitate to speak his honest conviction. He can say what he truly believes and never fear that any leak will bring future recriminations. Besides, each bishop is bound under mortal sin to vote only for such men as he believes before God are worthy of the episcopal office.

Here follows free and frank discussion with no holds barred. The future of the Church is at stake and everyone there knows it. Questions are asked, doubts settled, appraisals challenged, misunderstandings cleared up. For all that, some shoulders may still shrug and unimpressed heads dolefully shake. To this end each bishop is provided with three tokens for each vote. He has a white one for approval, a black one for rejection, and another color for abstention. This latter would be used if a bishop felt he did not know enough about the man to make an intelligent choice, pro or con.

As the discussion terminates, and the candidate's name is announced, each bishop drops his token (the irreverent imagination pictures it like a poker chip) into an urn. To ensure complete secrecy the two unused tokens are dropped into another urn. Then the tally is taken and the successful candidates are listed, beginning with the man who gets the most votes, and so on in order. This list is sent to the apostolic delegate in Washington, and to the proper Congregation in Rome. The latter is a kind of permanent commission concerned with supplying heads for vacant dioceses.

While some ambitious clergymen may grumble that few bishops die and none resign, what they really mean is that there is more available talent than there are available posts. It stands to reason that with such a meeting as we have described, occurring every two years, there are bound to be many more "seers" than sees. It is again somewhat like the army, where six men may languish as lieutenant colonels because the T.O. (Table of Organization) calls for only one colonel. On the other hand, the Church should thank God that there are so many more men adjudged worthy to govern a diocese than there are slots to absorb them.

One superb advantage of such a backlog of episcopal timber is not only its size but its variety. If the Vatican, for example, needed to fill a widowed diocese with a man who was between forty and fifty, who could speak Polish, who held a degree in canon law, and whose folks had been farmers (for an agricultural region), some bored official in the pertinent Congregation could probably push a few buttons on a computer and out would come a printout offering several candidates from which could be made a definite selection.

Did you ever wonder about the background of the average man who is designated as bishop? Is there a predictable pattern? A significant number of those who rule American dioceses emerge from the alumni of the North American College at Rome. In the clerical mind this seminary seems to have established itself as a sort of ecclesiastical West Point for the training of future officers of the Church in the U.S. It is not perhaps overtly intended to function as such; but since a fresh batch of brilliant students is sent there every year from diocesan seminaries throughout America, and since such red-sashed seminarians do have special opportunities to acquire degrees in Church sciences right in the heart of Christendom, these *Romani* have come to form an elite corps in the American Church. Their numbers have always provided an impressive quota of American bishops. Or, to put it another way, all American priests have Roman collars but comparatively few have Roman ties.

Perhaps a distinction should be made between the

head bishop of a diocese, who used to be called by the strange name of "ordinary" but is now simply the diocesan bishop, and the bishop appointed to assist him, who is called an auxiliary. Their backgrounds could be completely different. It is possible that the head bishop may often have had very little experience as a pastor in a parish. In many instances he spent his early years in a nonpastoral post such as secretary to another bishop, or as an official in the chancery, or as a professor in the seminary, or in an executive capacity in charge of the diocesan charities, or schools, or Propagation of the Faith: the dynasty of the desks.

Auxiliary bishops, on the other hand, may have passed many years of their priesthood in the anonymous routine of parish life. A goodly number of auxiliary bishops become diocesan bishops. By the way, not even an avant-garde liturgist could tell the diocesan bishop from the auxiliary by their vestments. Each wears a ring, each carries a crosier, and each is crowned with the towering headdress of the miter to indicate the fullness of the priesthood. Before the altar they are equal; it is at the desk where the difference lies. Both are empowered to confirm a Christian, to ordain a priest, to consecrate another bishop. But in the executive sphere the equality ceases. Only diocesan bishops can write pastoral letters, decide the boundaries of parishes, transfer personnel, and govern a diocese. You might almost say that the auxiliary bishop is only a resident guest in the diocese. Technically he is himself the bishop of *another* diocese, a diocese of long ago and far away and for the time suppressed.

But the auxiliary bishop has this consolation. He has all the honors connected with being a bishop and none of the headaches of ruling a diocese. Many a time the head bishop must feel that his miter is rightly shaped like a hornet's nest, buzzing with a hundred problems, and that his pectoral cross with all its massive gold and sparkling jewels is still very much a cross.

As a rule, the bishop of a diocese is a diocesan priest, though not necessarily a priest from that particular diocese. On the other hand, it is unusual for a member of a religious order — like a Jesuit or a Passionist or a Redemptorist — to become a bishop except in foreign mission lands. There are some exceptions, but those are in a definite minority. Such "order" priests have made solemn promises not to aspire to or to accept ecclesiastical honors. When the Holy See appoints such a one to a diocese (usually in the field afar), it automatically dispenses him from any contrary vow. Too, the chances are that many of the priests under the new bishop in that remote vineyard will belong to his own order anyway.

Ultimately, of course, the designation of each new bishop devolves upon the pope. But obviously — in a worldwide Church — he must depend on information funneled to him through local sources. The first of these is the process we have just described, which guarantees a permanent pool of capable men. Here comes step two, almost a carbon copy of what went before.

Once the funeral bells have tolled for a particular bishop, more immediate machinery begins to grind. In Washington the apostolic delegate will generally contact the archbishop of the bereaved province and probably some of its bishops requesting their suggestions. Even if he does not, they may write directly to Rome, recommending some man they feel especially qualified for that see. Meanwhile the apostolic delegate has selected three names from his episcopal file, and once more makes detailed secret inquiries about these finalists in a questionnaire that may range all the way from their mastery of foreign languages to their observance of the liturgy. So strict is the seal of silence imposed on those thus interviewed that any violation incurs an automatic excommunication which can be lifted only by the pope himself.

The full dossier on each of the three men under consideration might run to five thousand words. It is now up to the apostolic delegate to send these reports to the proper Congregation in Rome, and to list his own preferences — that is, he grades the men as first, second, third. When this reaches Rome, the Congregation there may decide to satisfy itself more thoroughly on some doubtful point, and proceed to conduct an independent investigation of its own.

One thing the Catholic Church has plenty of, and that is time. Generally months will have elapsed and the public will have forgotten all about the vacancy before anything happens. Even when the Roman Congregation decides on its appointee, it first seeks to learn through the apostolic delegate if the bishop-designate will accept. The Church is taking no chances on the public embarrassment that would ensue if a man rudely rejected a proffered miter.

Only now is the name of the "bishop-to-be" laid upon the pope's desk. This may look as if the manager has no say in the game till the ninth inning; but when you realize that there are almost one thousand dioceses in the Church plus the great number of auxiliary bishops, you can see that His Holiness cannot possibly be as well-informed as he would like to be on all candidates. He is only infallible, not omniscient — and therefore the details of the preliminary investigation must be made for him. Even at this juncture — if the pope believes in his deepest conscience that some other man (entirely an outsider or a dark horse) would fill the vacant bishopric better — he can veto all three names submitted and appoint instead a bright curate from South Snowshoe in the neighboring diocese, or from the other end of the country. This the Holy Father has the undisputed power to do, but just as indisputably rarely does. As a rule he goes along with the conveyor belt of protocol and its routine steps of nomination, investigation, designation, and — finally — papal confirmation.

To sum up: The process slides along like a ship going through a canal from lock to lock. First, there are the senior priests or the diocesan officials who answer the secret questionnaires about the candidate. Then there are the bishops from the province that ratify him, as well as the diocesan bishops who send in names for men they would like as their auxiliaries. (Two out of three bishops in this country begin as auxiliaries.) There is the Congregation for Bishops in Rome that discusses every case. And most of all, there is the apostolic delegate in Washington who perhaps has the strongest influence. Rome respects his judgment. When it does not, he is likely to be removed by way of a technical promotion. And of course at the very top of the pyramid is the pope. He may depend greatly on the wisdom of some particular archbishop or cardinal whose judgments he has come to respect.

Perhaps half the clerical conversation at a bishop's funeral is speculation, wistful, or fearful, about his successor. This interval — between the lowering of one man into the grave and the elevation of another to the throne — offers a field day for cagey deductions and wild surmises. Whose influence will predominate, whose views will prevail, whose protégé will be picked?

There were, alas, ages in the Church when God permitted the appointment of unworthy bishops for the same mysterious reasons that He allows earthquakes and leprosy. But by and large that day died with the divine right of kings. The most that can be alleged against the present procedure of selecting bishops in the United States is that it implies a self-perpetuating spiritual aristocracy.

But the sting goes out of this if you emphasize the word *spiritual*, with all its high and noble and sworn-to-God overtones. As to the aristocracy, the word means government by the best, and the Church has grimly tried to assure itself that these men are the best, both in intelligence and in integrity. (Prudence and discretion must be there too. Unbalanced genius or impetuous sanctity could ruin a diocese.)

Still, bishops are but men and not archangels, so the footprints of the human are bound occasionally to appear. A man in a miter who was without sin and without error would be a living heresy. But the general batting average is superb. Anyone who studies the magnificent record of the hierarchy in our country over the last half century — that is, since the present system of selecting bishops went into operation — must concede that the overall result is a towering monument both to the soundness of the method and to the quality of the men.

{ Seminary, Old Style }

To us it was a gloriously happy time, though perhaps the Pepsi generation would shake incredulous heads and brand it unreal ("it" being our life in the seminary sixty years ago, during the Roaring Twenties, the Age of Flaming Youth). Beyond the seminary gates, young people of our college age were then tilting hip flasks bubbling with illegal "hooch," dancing the Charleston, driving third-hand Stutz Bearcats, wearing raccoon coats to autumn stadiums, and even swallowing bowls of no-carat goldfish. They were talking excitedly about the first talking pictures, while we never left the seminary grounds to see even a silent picture.

For that matter, we never went to a restaurant, never had a cigarette, never heard a radio, never saw a magazine or a newspaper (we got important headlines from the faculty). Six years without making or receiving a phone call. Six years during which we slept under the same roof every single night, except for three nights in the fifth year when we went home to celebrate our first solemn Mass and perhaps three or four Saturday nights in the sixth year. On these weekends, we said Mass on Sunday to accommodate the summer crowds in Hudson Valley parishes. Our immediate family was allowed to visit us for one day three times a year or once a year for three days.

Our seminary was situated near a town with the strange name of Esopus. It was a huge gray granite building high above the lordly Hudson. Passengers on ships plying the river were impressed by its majestic structure but were a bit confused. Some were sure it was West Point; others held out for Sing Sing. On some depressing rainy afternoons we may have briefly thought the latter were right. But that was only a passing shadow floating across a tranquil, contented, and even enthusiastic life.

We spent our six weeks' vacation on the Hudson, picnicking in groups of twenty or so at various sites along the shore. One favorite spot was "Roosevelt's" at Hyde Park. We must have got clearance to go there, but the mansion seemed a mile away and we never saw anyone (possibly because we always left the place clean enough to get a *Good Housekeeping* seal). We cooked two meals every day, but the outcome was closer to C rations than to Julia Child or Escoffier. Sometimes a young voice might groan, "Who made that coffee?" And he would get a pastoral answer like "God made the coffee . . . and everything else."

On the way home we would sing, and it must have rung out pleasantly over the waters though it surely offered no threat to the Soldiers' Chorus at the Met. We had to be home by eight-thirty when everybody poured into chapel for night prayers, with monkish robes covering picnic togs. I can still remember kneeling in the pew, feeling I was swaying back and forth as if I were still in the boat. Night prayers were mercifully short, about ten minutes, and now when we climbed to our rooms and looked down on the darkening river, a line of oil barges might slide solemnly past; but since you could see only the lights, it looked like a procession of candles moving toward a shrine. In the morning the sun would make the water shimmer like gold pieces, or there might be a dim, melancholy mist. It was always the same water but never the same river.

If the seminary looked down on the Hudson, over on the other side the Sleeping Boy looked down on the seminary. The Sleeping Boy was what everybody called a long range of hills. Certainly in the fall, even to a cold realistic eye, it looked like a human figure slumbering under the multicolored afghan of autumn. The hikers among us would tramp through those hills on Sunday and Thursday afternoons, the times when we were free for athletics or long walks.

Some seminarians in this permissive age might think that, living the sheltered life we did, we should have come out of the seminary wearing not a Roman collar but a Buster Brown collar, and carrying not a Breviary but a large book of fairy tales. The truth is that our training was along the lines of a spiritual Marine boot camp. The program was grim; there was no nonsense; and you did what you were told. The doors, of course, opened from the inside and you could leave if you wanted. By then we had all made the year's novitiate, and if you got through that fine sieve, you generally stayed. A few left during the seminary course. A few were told to go. But by this time the vast majority of students had decided that the priesthood was the goal to which God had called them, and this was the steep path to that peak.

In our ordination class (1929), there were thirty-seven. It is sad to think that when you look at a picture of that group, there are only six of us left; but it is a happy thought to know that you do not have to mark an *X* across any young face, because they all were buried in their vestments or are wearing vestments now. That's the way it used to be. Stern training, but rich results.

You could describe seminary life as AAA (meaning Academics, Ascetics, and Athletics). Academically we had two sterling advantages: First, each man had his own room with long periods assigned to study; and secondly, the faculty were all members of our own religious order who were easily approachable for consultation and deeply interested in our progress. Curiously, a couple of the best had no graduate degrees, but a degree does not a teacher make. Experience and dedication made up for accreditation and kindled the fires in our minds. In later years, it was sad to see these faculty Fathers carried down the winding road under the weeping willows and laid side by side in the little cemetery near the pond that glows so often in the sunset like another miracle of water turned into wine.

I think of Father Hauser, who taught moral theology and whose wisdom flowed in a slow rich drawl; Father Green, who taught canon law and whose sharp mind went through a problem like an ice pick through cellophane; Father Leonard, who would look up from a page of Scripture and say something that made you think that angels were hovering in the room; Father Gounley, who taught philosophy and in whose brain burned a thousand-watt bulb and whom many of us almost blasphemously ranked right after the Father, Son, and Holy Spirit; and of course Father Francis Connell, who achieved international repute as a dogmatic theologian.

In his own specialty, Father John Waldron was as good as any one of them. He taught public speaking, the looked-down-upon stepchild in the intellectual family. Brisk, smiling, debonair, smartly groomed like an ad in an ecclesiastical magazine, he would sweep into the musty auditorium like a fresh breeze. He had charisma while that word was still buried in Greek dictionaries. His electric, dynamic approach stirred even the dullest. He could take your pitiful little homily and pour over it imagination and emotion so that it burst into crackling flames. May he, with all the others to whom we owe so much, rest in peace!

To get back to the academics, our studying was to a large extent confined to the assigned textbooks. You had to absorb these, but related material or background books were entirely up to you. In the world of general literature, our reading was severely but quietly restricted. Nowadays, accreditation demands all kinds of books, magazines, papers. In our day, this was nonexistent.

There was a large, handsome three-tiered library, but we had free access only to the lowest floor, which contained nothing but spiritual books. In six years, I never was on the two upper floors — or is it upper two floors? At any rate I never was there. If you wanted a book for other than pious reading (lives of the saints, etc.), you located the card in the file cabinet, wrote out a requisition slip, and handed it to the seminarian-librarian. If the Father-prefect approved, the book was left at your door. I never knew of a book not being approved, but I very much doubt that any of the best-sellers of that era (F. Scott Fitzgerald, Theodore Dreiser, Sherwood Anderson, Ernest Hemingway) would ever have found shelter on those monastic shelves.

Thus, by indirection, we were subtly directed toward the classics, a choice with which at this late date I heartily concur. A diet of Dickens, Scott, Thackeray, Macaulay, Stevenson, and the like ruled out indiscriminate reading and allowed us to escape literary herpes while promoting literary health. During vacations, when I felt especially wild, I would read O. Henry (William Sydney Porter) who, despite those trampoline endings, is much underrated.

It just occurs to me that in these marinated memories I have forgotten to say that our seminary was staffed by —

and conducted for — Redemptorists. The latter is admittedly an awkward word. It means a follower of the Redeemer, one who wants to do his little bit to spread the fruits of the Redemption. We Redemptorists are not the biggest religious order in the Church; we (if I may be allowed to boast) are merely the best. For an unbiased confirmation of that claim, just ask any unprejudiced Redemptorist.

In the three A's we were talking about, the second would stand for Ascetics — that is, the development of the spiritual life to balance the intellectual. In the seminary, they certainly tried to flood us with a love of God and the pursuit of virtue, study, and prayer. It was a calm, canal-like existence between those two banks, and the running lights were the desk lamp and the sanctuary lamp.

Incidentally, as in most institutions, the food was spartan. Everybody grumbled, but somehow everybody survived. One shock came my first Lent. I was only nineteen and not subject to the fast, but at supper everyone got his portion, the traditional eight ounces. One fishball, one dab of tomato sauce . . . whatever. Thanks be to God (and someone's common sense!) a dispensation came through the following year, and you could eat what you felt you needed.

Consider the rugged order of the day. Each morning at five an electric bell tore a screaming path down each corridor, and you stumbled out of bed to the cold concrete floor, dressed, then shaved and washed at your washstand with its huge porcelain pitcher and big white bowl. (There is no running water in any of the rooms of this Redemptorist rectory in Boston either, but we can shave and wash in the bathrooms. There were not enough sinks to do that in the seminary.) At 5:30, we gathered in the chapel for morning prayers, meditation, and Mass. Make your bed and set your room in order from 6:45 to 7:00. From

7:00 to 7:30, breakfast. There was no cooked food, so you were through in ten minutes.

During the day, we had another half hour of meditation, a half hour of spiritual reading, a rosary period, a visit to the Blessed Sacrament, and night prayers. We had a half day of silent retreat every week, one full day each month, and a block of five silent days twice a year. Every night in the seminary, "Lights out!" rang at ten. A light in any room showed through the transom like the aurora borealis and brought the Father-prefect to inquire if you were sick.

The final A of the AAA would be athletics, which were strictly intramural. We had baseball, basketball, handball, tennis, football — the touch variety made famous by the Kennedys. I write this with a sour smile, recalling how a priest who lived next to me in this rectory and whose soul has long since gone over the goalposts to God, suffered a broken jaw in "touch football." The teams were young and eager. Enthusiastic? Perhaps aggressive is the more precise term.

In our day there were one hundred and sixty seminarians, of whom forty were Canadians. We kept three ponds in action. How many tons of snow were shoveled, how often we dragged the crude barrel sleds to spray the ice! Oh, those happy, happy days in the Ten Acres hut when we gulped down mugs of steaming-hot but horrid coffee between periods! No wonder the faculty acidly observed that we majored in hockey and minored in theology.

What we learned in the seminary (the prayer, the preaching, the theology, the counseling) was put into practice in faraway places, from San Juan to Saskatchewan. The men whose youthful strides clacked along the long stone corridors of Mount Saint Alphonsus later climbed stairs in teeming tenements on New York's East Side, or slogged along past the hedgerows of Normandy or bounced in a jeep over hot trails in the Matto Grosso of Brazil.

Still, though they part at ordination for posts wide apart, whenever Redemptorists gather and reminisce, the talk always finds its way back to seminary days. This is the common denominator, the mutual experience dear to all. And it never seems that long ago back to the time when we knelt under the many-splendored stained-glass dome of the chapel while summer lightning flashed, or winter hail rattled its drums, or the March winds whined and howled. So many golden memories rest with folded wings amid those old pews, or on the dusty baseball diamond, or in the refreshing blue river, so clean in the 1920s that it lured you to hit the springboard hard and go diving in.

It was a hard but good life, and we loved it because it was preparing us for the priesthood, our life's goal — and because we were living shoulder to shoulder with men who had the same high aim, the same eager spirit, the same noble love for one another. Would I do it again? I sure would!

But I am eighty now, so I hope the Lord taps some young fellow on the shoulder to take my place. You don't have to be bright. Just willing.

{ Excommunication? }

One blustery January afternoon in the eleventh century, Pope Gregory VII paced back and forth in a high-vaulted room in the castle of Canossa. Later Gregory was to be canonized as a saint and enshrined in history as Hildebrand (as unlikely a name as any for an Italian Benedictine monk), but at the moment he was only plucking at the velvet drapes with his long fingers and staring down into the winter courtyard. A wild wind from the Apennines was whirling great white flakes, like the ghosts of summer butterflies, across the landscape. Down in the courtyard the members of a king's retinue huddled, stamped, and cursed under their frosty breaths. In the very center, booted and spurred — stamping as much from a slow burn as from the cold — was the king himself, Henry IV, emperor of Germany.

The king with the cold feet and the hot head was an impetuous monarch in his twenties who had broken with the tradition of former emperors, like Constantine and Clovis and Charlemagne, by pushing a program that called for the Church to serve him (the State), instead of the State serving the Church. Specifically, he insisted on the right to appoint the bishop in every diocese of his empire — even in the face of the scandalous fact that this had meant auctioning miters for money, and making shepherds of the flock a number of men who in their private lives were ravenous wolves or, at best, fawning puppies cringing at the emperor's throne.

For the general good of the Church, Pope Gregory (a man with a heart of oak and a will of steel) declared that this system was venal and vicious and forthwith must be abolished. The impetuous and power-mad Henry countered by declaring that Gregory VII was no longer the legitimate pope. Gregory retaliated by thundering an excommunication. (In the history books all excommunications are thundered, just as in journalism all footballs thud and all chests are thumped.) In any event, the Supreme Pontiff excommunicated the emperor, and, in order to have this censure lifted, Henry had to come to Canossa.

For two hours Gregory had let Henry cool his heels — literally! — in the snowy courtyard, because the pope knew that the whole medieval world was watching. There was nothing personal or picayune about the delay. It was in every sense coldly official and solely directed by a sense of duty. Gregory was a man of granite who was giving the king who had "deposed" him a king-size lesson that his imperial memory would not soon forget. But now Gregory looked out for the last time, closed the drape, and nodded to an aide.

A few moments later, a lock rattled downstairs, a snow-dusted cloak dropped on the stone stairs, and footsteps came bounding up. To the pope's surprise the blond young king bent his knee before the silver-haired churchman, and immediately the pontiff took the spoiled young monarch into his arms, led him over to the cozy fire, gave him a goblet of warming wine, and an hour or so later in solemn ceremony absolved Henry from the excommunication.

This was perhaps the most celebrated excommunication in history. When an excommunication is of international prominence with names named, as in the instance of Elizabeth of England or Luther of Germany, novelists and dramatists love to serve it up as a full-course book or play. Bulwer-Lytton used even the mere threat of excommunication effectively in his *Richelieu*, where the tall figure with the aristocratic gray goatee in the flaming cardinal's robe took his walking stick and traced a solemn circle in the dust around himself and majestically threatened that the awesome weight of excommunication would fall upon anyone so rash as to lay hands upon his person. "Here I draw the sacred line of Rome. . ." — and when Walter Hampden drew the line and bit out the words back in the 1930s, the hairs crinkled on the back of your neck.

But in our atomic age, when Church and State have long since walked their separate ways (a blessed boon in practice if not the theological ideal), what about this matter of excommunications? Do they have any muscle beyond the mouth that utters them? Are they practical? Do they ever affect little people whose names never see headlines?

Literally, excommunication — if you dissect the word — means being cut off from the community. Ecclesiastically, it means being excluded from the body of the Church. Certainly it is a logical practice. If students can be expelled from a college, and members dropped from a club, and servicemen dishonorably discharged from the armed forces — then surely any of the members of the faith who are not faithful to their Church in a grave matter can be cut off, or excommunicated, from membership in that Church. Heretics, for example, because they hold doctrines at variance with the truth, are excommunicated. (That schoolboy meant well, but did not have it precisely right, when he wrote that Luther did not die a natural death but was excommunicated by a papal bull.)

Any respectable society has the right to set up conditions for membership therein, and also to cast adrift those who refuse to meet its requirements. No society could exist without this right, and outsiders who presume to dictate the standards of membership are merely presumptuous. The Jews practice excommunication, as witness the case of Spinoza. Even the Quakers, or Friends, have invoked it. What of course gives the Church special assurance is that there still echoes in its ears the voice of Christ: "He who will not hear you, let him be to you as the heathen and the publican." And, "What you shall bind upon earth is also bound in heaven." The Church is a society that is different. It is divine, of God.

In the language of the canon lawyers, the usual purpose of excommunication is medicinal rather than punitive. Translated into Brooklynese, this means that excommunications are pronounced more in sorrow than in anger, and even more in hope than in sorrow. In other words, the Church levels its excommunication at a man not because the Church is enraged at the man's crime but because it is heartbroken at that man's spiritual condition. It pities him to the extent that it wants to shock him back to his senses by a stiff condemnation. Excommunication is something like the sharp resounding slap on the face that a mother might give her daughter to bring her out of hysteria. It is prompted not by hate but by love. What the Church seeks is always the good of the sinner, for him to realize the enormity of the evil, renounce his error, change his conduct for the better, and return to the bosom of the fold.

May we point out here that no excommunication can ever take from a man his status as a Christian? Once a man is baptized, his soul is stamped with the seal of that sacrament forever — and no sin of his, no excommunication of the Church, can blot this out or even blur it. What excommunication *can* do is lay upon a man a brand like the brand of Cain, a stigma that makes him an exile from his spiritual home. It is so terrible a penalty that, as long as the offender chooses to be obstinate, in the eyes of the Church he does not even exist. It is as if across his mail were scrawled the ultimate rejection, "Unknown."

What actions (or nonactions) would cause an individual to be excommunicated today? Certainly far fewer than in the old days. The new version of canon law is strong for just punishments, censures, and interdicts but goes comparatively light on excommunications. Here are some of the present sad cases that rate automatic excommunication:

- If you abandon the true faith for heresy.
- If you give your children to be raised in a heretical sect.
- If you dare to attack physically the person of the pope.
- If you throw away the Sacred Host.

- If you procure an abortion.

Similarly a bishop incurs excommunication if he consecrates a priest a bishop without papal mandate. A priest incurs excommunication if he directly violates the seal of confessional secrecy.

However, a man incurs an excommunication only if he knows that this penalty is attached to his action. This does not mean that he has to know the technical canonical details about the penalty. It is enough (for example, in the case of abortion) that the person know that not only is the action a mortal sin against God's law but that it also carries with it some sort of grave penalty imposed by the Church.

But where is the bite in excommunication? How sharp are its teeth? What punishments will the excommunicated feel? Certainly there will be no midnight pounding on a man's door, no prodding with a bayonet as he is hustled into a freight car for a long, crammed, and shivering ride to Siberia. In excommunication, the penalties are real; but rather than physical they are spiritual. For instance, the excommunicated person (say the woman who procures an abortion) is forbidden to receive Holy Communion. Strictly speaking she has no right to attend Mass. She can gain no indulgences. She can expect (if she dies unrepentant) no church funeral, or burial in consecrated ground. Curiously, one thing not forbidden to the excommunicated is attendance at sermons. Could it be that this is considered a subtle species of punishment?

But suppose the excommunicated wishes to come back. How does the prodigal, now beyond the pale, set about returning to his Father's house? He has but to knock at the door and (unlike the king of Canossa) only once. The man, for example, who has thrown away the Sacred Host need but go to confession, repent of his sin, and he can be restored to the bosom of the Church. In certain excommunications, the priest must appeal to the bishop for the power to absolve. In that case there is of course no disclosure of names. Secrecy is preserved by the filing of what amounts to a John Doe petition for the removal of the excommunication. But the very necessity of the appeal to a higher power emphasizes to the penitent the gravity of the offense. Of course, where the penitent is dying, any priest can absolve from any excommunication — if the person promises (if he survives) to obey the violated law in the future.

This matter of excommunication is not a pleasant subject. But as Christ of the knotted cords whipped the money changers out of the temple, so the Church that He founded has to drive out, albeit much more gently, those who mock its laws. The door, however, that shuts out the excommunicated is never locked. It opens easily from the outside.

{ Roman Holiday }

I made the mistake of dropping in at the office of our diocesan weekly to borrow something and came away with a request for a piece on the Boston pilgrimage to Rome for the canonization of Saint John Neumann. The editor implied that he wanted what the wire services would not provide, namely the unimportant and unreported details, the little homely happenings — not the towering pyramid of the great event but the tiny sands of minor incidents; a bunt, not a homer.

Well, we made the trip over and back in a transatlantic flying bus they call a 707. It was crammed to capacity. The seats were three abreast, lined on either side of an aisle so narrow that you had to inhale if you met someone coming the other way. There was no first-class section, so the cardinal and the five other members of the hierarchy had the same rugged seating as the "lower-archy" for the eight hours we were in the air (the "lower-archy" consisting of several priests, a fair sprinkling of religious, and the solid core of pilgrim laity, which brought the total to one hundred and eighty).

In the whole party there were (I think) only two children: a girl and a boy. The lad was assigned with his mother to our hotel, and in the course of various safaris I found out that if you do not want to miss anything, bring either binoculars or a boy. Youngsters don't miss a trick. Ask any magician.

Ours was, of course, a chartered tour, and once you tied that triple knot on your baggage tag, and surrendered your luggage, you became a helpless yo-yo in the hands of the travel agency. By taking "a tour" you save a lot of money, but you lose your freedom. In a week's trip like ours, it is the frantic pace that surprises you: Boston, Rome, Naples, Capri, Pompeii, Sorrento, Naples, Rome, Shannon, Boston. . . . At the end you know how an egg feels in that whirling, swirling eggbeater.

I suppose it has to be that way. Our guide, for example, announced that we could leave the bus for ten minutes so as to walk down the long street and admire the Trevi Fountain. He pointedly added, "I mean ten American minutes, not Roman minutes." Apparently Roman minutes are graciously elastic. Precision is for brain surgeons; relaxation is for Romans. But if in Rome you do what the Romans do, you will miss the American bus. At any rate, it is a pleasant attitude.

Some things about another country you are bound to love; other things annoy your American-tooled outlook. You love the hotel bath towels that seem two miles long and a half-mile wide. Then you look at the bar of yellow soap, so small that a child might take it for an appealing piece of butterscotch.

Any traveler knows that a sojourn in another country (even for a week, like our tour) is bound to be a strange blend of delights and disappointments, of brief ecstasies and lingering exasperations. You come upon scenes so gorgeous that you are convinced you are looking at a postcard or a calendar. You stand before ruins that make you feel that you are reaching across the ages and touching fingertips with history. And then the bubble breaks with a frustrating wait for a bus that has broken down, or a long stand on a hot pier squinting across the blistering Bay of Naples for a ship that doesn't come in.

I am sure the last thing that any of the pilgrims expected in connection with the canonization of Saint John Neumann was to become seasick, but about thirty of them gave up everything but the ghost. That was on the way to the Isle of Capri.

During our week we traveled by plane, ship, bus, trolley, taxi. Some took side trips on trains, and I suppose a few clip-clopped along the cobbled streets in open carriages. To the shrine of Canterbury the medieval pilgrims cantered long ago, giving us the word for that leisurely gait, or canter. What word do you use, though, to describe a pilgrimage in a jet six miles above the earth and streaking along at six hundred miles an hour?

Spade-bearded old Chaucer could probably swivel his sharp eyes, and tilt his keen ears, and then start his quill scratching out a new bundle of tales about pilgrims in the atomic age. I just don't have his equipment. In our tour groups I had expected to see singular types, like the blusterer in the crowd, who cannot be happy unless he is also loud. Or the somber one, pursed of lip and prim of speech, who identifies dignity with silence. Perhaps even a timid soul, so frightened that she does her flying with a rosary in one hand and a martini in the other. There may have been characters like these among the whole one hundred and eighty, but I certainly did not see them. When we reached Rome we were divided into three groups at different hotels, and rarely — if ever — saw one another during the whole week.

Our group (and there is no reason to believe the other two sections were cut from different cloth) was a quiet, happy, pleasant crowd, good-humored even during bad times, tolerant when things were rough. They could have risen up in righteous wrath on more than one occasion when poor planning stood out like a Roman obelisk. But they remembered they were pilgrims who came here out of personal love for the new saint, and they passed off disappointments with a shrug and a smile. They were, in fact, so good that they shamed me into never revealing that on several occasions I was a dormant volcano.

We were, in the main, a company of senior citizens. One lovely lady with a cane said to me toward the end of the week, "Father, you keep up with us very well." That night I looked in the mirror hard.

There was (as I mentioned) a sixth-grade boy among us who unconsciously taught us all a lesson. We had just come groping out of the cool darkness of the catacombs of Saint Callistus, and nearby there waved a field of wheat with flaming poppies nodding between the rows. In the bus the guide had started his usual count. "One missing," he said. At that moment young David burst in, and handed his mother a poppy. "For you, Mom." Not many lads that age would think of a gesture like that. It reflected well on the mother as well as on the boy.

Speaking of guides, on one occasion ours was a genial Roman matron who was constantly referring to the great basilica as that of "Saint Mary *the* Major." This sent my undisciplined mind thinking about "General" absolution, "Corporal" works of mercy, and "Private" interpretation. Well, we are the Church militant, are we not?

In this connection, though, I wonder what bilingual Italians thought when they heard a gentleman (though hardly a scholar) saying that he had come to Rome before on the "Attila Airlines." This should not happen even to a Hun.

Everything you have heard about Roman traffic is true. The *topolini* (or little mice, as the Italians call their tiny cars) bear down on you at every intersection like a column of fire ants. Compared to the traffic at a Roman intersection, Ben Hur's chariot race was a languid dawdle on a suburban road. I never crossed the whizzing street without sending up a swift prayer for protection to Saint John Neumann, and when I emerged on the other side (breathing hard but still in one piece) I thanked him heartily for another miracle. In a cab (that darting, twisting, misguided missile) I would invoke another American saint, Mother Cabrini, feeling that cabs might come under her jurisdiction. Any port in a storm, and any patron in a predicament.

You have heard your fill, I suppose, about the majesty of Saint Peter's, so vast that to maintain harmonious proportion, the quill in the hand of Saint Mark has to be five feet long. In the rear of Saint Peter's is Michelangelo's touching "Pietà," with our Lady holding in her lap the dead Christ. I love the classic beauty of our Lady's face; but I have always felt that her shoulders, wider even than those of Jesus, are too broad to be in proportion. When I asked the guide about this, he scowled at me as if I had attacked our Lady's virtue instead of merely her image. Has anyone ever heard this discussed elsewhere, or am I a solitary, sour killjoy?

Rome is also, to be sure, the Sistine Chapel (rarely used as a chapel — mostly a museum with a halo) where you marvel at the swirl of colors on either wall, and having stared at the dramatically flamboyant ceiling, you leave as stiff-necked as any Pharisee. But what a glorious, thrilling spot!

On your way out you may glimpse a Swiss Guard looking just like himself on a postcard in that uniform of eye-dazzling blue and red and gold. If you like uniforms, you will love Italy. The ordinary policeman with his trimly tailored white jacket looks like the maître d'hôtel of any ritzy restaurant.

Speaking of police, the unanimous opinion in our particular group was that we could walk the streets of Rome far more securely than those of rugged Roxbury. However, I heard that a couple of women in the other two groups had their purses snatched, but there was no personal injury.

Our Redemptorist habit (or cassock), I was thinking, on the way to the canonization ceremony, is the complete rebuttal to any pickpocket. His gliding hand would soon be lost in the long, dark depths of those mini-shaft pockets. Pickpockets, they say, love canonizations. I wonder: Were there any prowling about and plying their deft craft at the Crucifixion?

Of all Roman churches, the dearest to Redemptorists has to be that of San Alfonso (where the priests of our party concelebrated Mass for the pilgrims). We all agreed that the original picture of Our Mother of Perpetual Help, enshrined there, seems smaller than our copy at the Mission Church. But to kneel here was like coming to the source of the river, because all other pictures are only tributaries.

In this church, as in all others where we said Mass for the pilgrims, we had a silent understanding with one man in our party to take up the collection. His wife made the ultimate sacrifice: surrendering her handsome straw bonnet as a collection basket, into which the lire poured. Curiously, in every case when we turned over the hat filled with those dirty, raggedy bills to the sacristan of the church we were using, he invariably thought that the straw hat went with the collection. To which we said in strange English, "Lire, yes; lid, no."

The only Romans we found impossible were the men who pushed rosaries and medals under your nose on the street, or who showed you a "gold" bracelet, half hidden in its paper wrappings. These were aggressive, pushy, bold — the ignoblest Romans of them all.

In the streets approaching Saint Peter's it was a personal pleasure for me to hear the vendors call the new saint "Saint John Newman" (to rhyme with "human") instead of "Noimann," when they offered their Neumann medals, pictures, statues, and the like. Mercifully the Neumann ashtrays, thermometers, and cushions were not available when our group was in Rome. (Incidentally, the pope — both at the canonization and at the general audience — always called the saint "Newman," except when addressing the Germans.)

As we came to Saint Peter's Square for the ceremonies that bright Sunday morning, the tall semicircle of pillars they call the Bernini Colonnade seemed like two giant arms outstretched in warm welcome. As the morning went on, that warm welcome soared to torrid. They tell me it was not so bad in the square itself where the laity were seated, but up on our exposed platform the air was broiling. When a rare cloud floated across the sun you could see heads tilt up and give thanks for a moment's relief in the fiery furnace.

The papal altar was in the center of the raised platform. On one side were the massed cardinals and bishops in their red robes looking like a grounded sunset. On the other side was the Redemptorist contingent. We had come from five continents and from twenty-nine countries to honor our confrere, the new saint. On my right was a Redemptorist from Vietnam; on my left, one from Canada;

the man in back of me was from Copenhagen; and the man in front, from Brazil. We have our own United Nations, but under God.

The inevitable camera bugs (even among the clergy) leaped up on the benches and snapped their greedy shutters while the cry came from those in back, "Down in front!" It could have been Fenway Park. As Redemptorists we had a prominent spot, and therefore could be seen, but not an advantageous spot from which to see. Occasionally my eyes would drift up to the papal apartments right behind us where two old nuns of the Holy Father's household were looking down with the ideal view for the whole spectacle.

Saint Peter's Square — and not Saint Peter's Basilica — was the site of the canonization for the practical reason that it could accommodate more people. Yet I secretly longed for what used to be, when canonizations were held in Saint Peter's itself. We missed the long, colorful procession ranging from sandal-footed Capuchins to crimson-robed canons. And the silver trumpets blaring from the lofty balconies. And the bells of Rome tumbling in their towers. And the dome of Saint Peter's draped with strings of gleaming electric bulbs like strings of pearls.

But something like that costs and costs. Anyway, ours is liturgically a simpler age, and by sheer coincidence the bells of Saint Peter's boomed the hour of ten at the very moment when the pontiff was proclaiming John Newmann a saint, and they boomed eleven precisely as the pope lifted high the Sacred Host at the Consecration.

An hour later — to the chiming of the Angelus bell — Pope Paul stood at a window of his apartment and led the people in that age-old prayer to our Lady. Did somebody say the Church was downgrading devotion to Mary? The head of the Church certainly is not!

The only time Saint John Neumann came to Rome

was to honor our Lady on that happy day of the proclamation of the Immaculate Conception. "I thank God," he wrote, "that He has allowed me to see this day!" From Rome he journeyed as a pilgrim to Mary's shrine at Loreto near the Adriatic. In Vienna he preached on our Lady twice. When he returned to Philadelphia he asked every Catholic church in his diocese to hold a special triduum in honor of Mary Immaculate. So you can see that his devotion to her was deep and vibrantly alive.

How surprised Saint John Neumann would have been to see these thousands upon thousands of people centering in on Rome from all over Christendom to do him honor! Is it not a marvel in itself that one little man could bring so many together and from so far? Does it not show the democracy of the Catholic Church that this immigrant who landed on our American shores wearing a shabby suit, with one crumpled dollar in his pocket, should be officially recognized for the great man he was?

None of us who attended the canonization can ever be indifferent to him hereafter. If one master key in a hotel can open hundreds of doors, the influence of a man like Saint John Neumann can influence tens of thousands of hearts.

And we saw it all happen in Rome. There is no place like Rome. But, in another sense, there is no place like home either.

chapter seven

SILHOUETTE OF THE SAVIOR

{ **Born in a Cave, Died on a Hill** }

Some of us can remember when during Passiontide the church looked like a convention of hunched purple ghosts. The statues, the crucifixes, and the pictures were draped in somber violet. Why this was so was never quite clear — unless perhaps during this sacred time the Church wanted us to think less about the saints and more about the suffering Savior. But why then was the crucifix also veiled in violet? Was it to remind us to think not of the crucifix but of the cross, the original cross with the Figure sagging and writhing in final pain?

To look upon that cross with all its horror and shock, the reality of the death-sweat and the dripping blood, is not something for the queasy. Certainly it is not for the token Christian who just goes through the motions. But for the man who approaches Good Friday heartbroken about his past but resolute about his future, the cross is of all pulpits the most tender and most consoling. It is the guarantee of God's forgiveness signed in blood.

Suppose, then, this is the brown hill of Calvary and we are there. At long last the Christ who was born in a cave, carried across a desert, reared in a village, tempted on a mountain, baptized in a river, who walked on a lake and was betrayed in a garden — this same Christ is about to die on a small obscure hill. But first His garments must be torn off. Crucifixion is not a full-dress affair — it is an obscene insult. By law the condemned man's clothing goes to the executioners. We are prone to forget that in earlier days apparel was far more valuable than it is today. It was made by hand and it was made to last. From King Alfred to Queen Elizabeth I, you will find bequests of cloaks and bonnets in English wills. Shakespeare left his clothes to his nephews.

Very probably our Lady had woven her Son's robe herself. How she would have wanted it as a relic! But now rough hands rip it from His back. Still, it does not come off easily. The blood of the scourging has clotted, and shreds of scarlet flesh come peeling off with the heavy cloth. Soon dice will be clicking as the soldiers gamble for the garment of God.

Meanwhile, He stands there, all but naked, before that coarse and ribald crowd. The saints have never doubted that this agony of silent, sensitive shame was the price the Savior had to pay to atone for mankind's shameless sins of the flesh. What a huge, slimy, crawling cesspool these vices would make if you could throw them altogether: all the world's indecent thoughts and looks, all the pictures and books, all the jests and songs and deeds! Is it not true that the road away from God is generally a *dirt* road? Do not most people drop down into hell through the trapdoor of impurity?

Perhaps one of the soldiers now seizes the stripped Figure and snarls, "You have had a long walk and carried a heavy load, so you must be tired. Why not lie down (you are already undressed) and get a little rest?" With that he flings our Lord flat upon the heavy planks. There is no struggle, but others are there to hold Him down. The chief executioner drops to one knee beside Him. The sharp point of the long blue nail touches the palm which involuntarily quivers. The hammer swings back and crashes down through ribboned flesh, through crunching bone and spurting blood.

Is it any wonder that our Savior's head instinctively turns away? And where are those wide agonizing eyes looking, but straight at us, as if pleading for mercy? This is not just imagination or sentiment or rhetoric. Christ was crucified, not so much on Mount Calvary, as on Mount Sin. If there was no sin, there never would have been a Calvary. The popular spiritual is right in asking, "Were you there when they crucified my Lord?" Which of us can honestly answer, "No!" Saint Paul solemnly implies that every serious sin crucifies Jesus Christ anew.

Now that He has been spread out and nailed down, the idea is to get Him up there for the mob's amusement. Slowly, the cross is pushed up and up, till it falls with a shock into the prepared hole. That sudden drop almost tears our Lord's body from the spikes. So, He begins His long death-agony, hanging between heaven and earth. He had come down from heaven to redeem the earth, and now — having left the one and been rejected by other — He is cruelly suspended between both. No figure in all history is so forlorn as that half-naked Man spread out against the hilltop sky. No man ever left this world seeming so empty-handed a failure. In either hand He had nothing to show for His life but the blood-crusted head of a spike over which His limp fingers feebly closed.

Not at all a pretty picture, and not at all like those daintily artistic crucifixes in the religious-article stores. The thorns and the nails are digging into Him; the merciless sun is beating down upon Him; the sweat is pouring in streams off Him; the blood is dripping out of Him; the dust tramped by the crowd is swirling around Him; the mocking voices are shouting their cruel taunts at Him, like dogs snapping at a treed animal, or like wolves howling for the blood of the Lamb of God.

For three hours that seemed more like three centuries, Mary was in the midst of this. She heard His last words, when He forgave His executioners and, as His last will and testament, bequeathed her to mankind as its spiritual Mother. Then slowly a weird green light crept over the land. The great eye of the sun went bloodshot at what it had to see. In the unnatural darkness, the songs of the birds went silent. A clap of thunder like the beat of a huge drum vibrated the air, shook the hill, split the rocks, tore the sacred veil of the temple from top to bottom, and opened the very tombs.

But none of this matters. The important thing is that with one last shuddering convulsion the gaunt Figure on the cross stiffened and died. Sophisticates have sneered that "God is dead." No, He is not dead, but He did die that day, died to atone for our sins and to save us from the punishment of eternal death; and to prove that He could do this, He rose gloriously from the grave.

With our Lady, we look up at the cross, with sorrow of course, but also with reassurance. Could there be a more fitting symbol of salvation and forgiveness? His arms are outstretched, wide enough to embrace the world. They are fastened tight, meaning those redeeming arms will always stay open. It does not matter how low a man has fallen, how far he has strayed, how long he has been away. If only he comes crawling back to the cross for pardon, the arms of a merciful Jesus are always stretched out wide to welcome him!

Not just to welcome, but to forgive, for He has atoned for all our sins. Back in the fifteenth century when Henry, prince of Wales, was a young man carousing with Falstaff, he disgraced the royal name with his wild behavior. Everybody knew him for an idler, a drunkard, a libertine. Then rebellion broke out in the North against his father, King Henry IV. Overnight the dissolute prince became a different man. He went to the king, raised his sword in salute, and said, "Father, I know that by my gross ways I have sinned against you. But I go now to fight in your behalf. Before I return, this arm may well be smeared with my blood. But when I wash off that blood, I shall be also washing off my evil days and my shame!"

We too have sinned against our Father, God. But we do not have to wash away these sins with our blood. His divine Son has already done that for us. All we have to do is to be sorry, to come to the cross and ask forgiveness. Now is the time to do it, because this crucified Jesus cannot — will not — punish us. His hands are tied. Tied? They are nailed. And His heart is wide open, opened with a lance. On Good Friday the cross was all horror. Now it is all hope. His death is the symbol of outstretched mercy, the pledge of our eternal life.

{ Loaves and Fish }

Every year we hear the Gospel about the loaves and fish, and the tendency is to be piously bored. We shouldn't, of course, and wouldn't, if we listened with our minds and our hearts instead of just with our ears. Like a master's painting, a scriptural scene demands more than a passing glance. I have no doubt that a tourist in Rome could visit Michelangelo's "Last Judgment" every day for a week and each day discover something that had hitherto escaped him.

The general lesson to be lifted from the multiplication of the loaves and fish is the compassion of Christ, His consideration for the crowd, His pity for the common, hungry people. At Cana He had provided drink; here He furnishes food, two different outpourings of His love for human beings. Isn't that why He became one Himself, to love and to be loved? Christ loved us enough to be born a helpless baby, squirming within the four rough boards of a crib, and to die a tortured man writhing on the two splintery planks of the cross. Now on the hilltop, He tilts His loving, compassionate face toward the needs of the multitude.

To absorb the whole range of this incident, you must go to different Evangelists. Together they make the scene come alive. You learn that our Lord turned to Philip (who came from that region and knew the territory) and suggested to him that the Apostles go to the nearest villages and buy the bread. Christ, of course, knew what He was going to do, and must have smiled at Philip's precise analysis of the situation. "Feed this crowd?" Philip said in effect. "Why it would take two hundred denarii!" A denarius was a Roman coin and was the daily wage of a laborer. Scripture scholars have since researched the price of a loaf in those days, and have concluded that two hundred denarii would have purchased about forty-eight hundred loaves. Since the Gospel mentions five thousand men there, it was much better than a ball-park estimate.

A Jewish loaf of bread in those days was not oblong like ours, but round, looking something like a huge roll. Some biblical commentators believe that when the devil said to Christ in the desert, "If you are the Son of God, turn these stones into bread," he had in mind that the large round stones resembled the shape of Jewish bread. At any rate, it was barley bread because this was the bread of the poor. The rich man's bread was made of wheaten flour.

Andrew must have heard our Savior speaking to Philip, because very diffidently he approached Christ and said, "There is a boy here with five loaves and two dried fish. But" — and you can almost hear the helplessness in his voice — "what are these among so many?"

There may have been even scorn in his tone of voice. But there was no scorn in Christ's words when He must

125

have said, "Bring the lad here." And, with the lad's little, the Lord did much. He always does. He always can. We may not have much in our basket of talents: no artistic ability, no computer brain, no captivating personality — it does not matter. What the Lord looks for is goodwill, sincerity, spirit. He can take what in itself is a neighbor to nothing and by His power use it to achieve wonders.

Look what He did with Saul, the bigot bent on destroying the very name Christian. But Christ saw in Saul the conviction of a man who followed his conscience, misguided as it then was, and transformed him from Saul into Paul, the "Thirteenth Apostle." Or consider Ignatius Loyola — an army officer who was worldly, but whose basic instincts were right — and out of this material Christ formed the founder of the Jesuit Order. Or think of Camillus de Lellis, a compulsive gambler. What sleazy fabric out of which to make a saint! But Camillus became a saint and the patron of hospitals. Matt Talbot was a compulsive drinker, an alcoholic, who came to Christ saying, "All I have is disgust with myself and a need for you." By the grace of God this Dublin drunkard bounced from the gutter to the stars. His cause for canonization is on its way.

With anyone's basket of little, our Lord can do a lot. But first we have to bring the basket to Him and ask.

The miracle of the loaves and fish stands up as a forecasting of the Mass. The hill is the high altar. The boy is the server. The Apostles with the baskets going among the crowd are the priests with the ciboriums going along the altar rail. The people spread over the grass in groups of fifty and wearing the bright garments of that day are the congregation. Seated on the grass in their bright cloaks, they must have looked like flower beds or stained-glass windows.

The footnote to the story has its own point. After the miracle was over, the Apostles gathered up twelve baskets of fragments. Now no one could ever say, "We imagined all this. It was only an illusion." Not with all those crusts left over.

And the fish too were there for a purpose. Most modern Christians are unaware how far the fish goes back in Christian history or symbolism. In the catacombs you will find images of fish, crudely carved images of fish, on the tombs of martyrs. Most of the first converts to Christianity were Greek. The Greek word for fish is an acronym, each letter standing for a word, with the words translating into: "Jesus Christ, Son of God, Savior." In the days of persecution, if a Christian thought the man he was speaking to might be a Christian like himself, he would idly trace with his staff on the ground the form of a fish. This was the Christian countersign.

What was only foreshadowed about the Eucharist in the miracle of the loaves is realized in every Mass. There we have the real Bread of Life, Manna, the Bread come down from heaven. "This is My Body. . . . Do this in memory of Me." It is He whom we meet and receive into ourselves at Holy Communion.

How humbly we should receive Him! They say that Charlemagne, who was crowned emperor of France by the pope on Christmas Day in the year 800, was so impressed with his own importance that he gave instructions about his interment that makes one raise an incredulous eyebrow. He reasoned that when he died and went to heaven, it would be like one king meeting another, so he wanted to do so in state. He was therefore buried seated on a throne, a crown on his head and a scepter in his hand, and on his knees the great book of laws of his kingdom. Vanity has never been lowered to such heights.

From the absurd arrogance of Charlemagne we should learn to meet Christ at the communion rail humbly. (Incidentally, would that all communion rails were back and that the God-Man was received kneeling as befits His eminence and our lowliness!) But what of those who dare to receive Him with a soul stained by serious sin? This is like scornfully tossing a gorgeous, scarlet velvet rose on a heap of garbage, or idly dropping a Tiffany diamond into a barrel of trash.

He is Jesus, our God, our Savior, our Lord, so we must receive Him humbly, purely, pleasingly — pleading for the special graces we need. Centuries ago when the Turks laid siege to Vienna, and the inhabitants were slowly starving, King John Sobieski of Poland arrived with his army. But before he engaged the enemy he insisted that his troops have the opportunity to go to confession and receive Holy Communion. Only then did he lead them against a Turkish force that outnumbered his army three times to one. It was David against Goliath, but once more God was with David.

After the victory he wrote his brief communique to the pope, taking a leaf from Julius Caesar's *"Veni, vidi, vici"* ("I came, I saw, I conquered"). King John wrote, *"Veni, vidi, Deus vicit!"* — "I came, I saw, God conquered!" We can conquer too, against that triple alliance of the world, the flesh, and the devil, if we beg at Holy Communion for the specific graces we need. If we bring our basket (light and little as it is) to the Lord, He can — as He did with the five loaves and two fish — make much out of little, and even bring victory out of defeat.

{ Carpenter Among Fishermen }

In New Orleans they call it *Mardi Gras*, the "Fat Tuesday" that precedes lean Lent. In Rio it is *Carnival*, or "Farewell to Meat." And in the old days it really was. White-haired Father Jasinski used to tell us young priests that, when he was a boy in nineteenth-century Poland, his home never saw one scrap of meat during the entire six weeks of Lent. By contrast, our American Lent has melted down from a snowman to a snowflake. Now we are enjoined to refrain from meat only on Lenten Fridays.

As a rule, March is the fishiest time of the year. It used to be much worse. Not too long ago the Catholic calendar (courtesy of some funeral director) showed the page for March with the little squares for the dates like so many little white pools, each floating its tiny black fish, solemnly admonishing that this was a day of abstinence, with meat permitted only at the evening meal. It is surprising that then (before our present jolly ecumenical era), Protestants would good-humoredly refer to us Catholics as "fish eaters" or "mackeral snappers." I wonder how many of them recognized our Friday fish as a gesture of penance for sin, a splinter from the cross of the first Good Friday.

Though I am a thousand light-years removed from sanctity, I liked it better then when in those grim days every Friday of the year was a meat no-no. For one thing, it made you do that little bit of penance every week, on schedule. Most of us do not have a Catholic stomach, and prefer hamburgers to haddock and corned beef to cod, so it was at least a minor mortification. Oh, I know you could also have baked stuffed lobster, but how many could afford that?

Secondly, fish on Friday reminded you that you belonged to the lodge, that you were a Catholic. It proclaimed and promoted solidarity. Of course, this could be overplayed. A man once told me of a Boston Catholic executive who went to New York for a weekend with his young Catholic secretary. That Friday evening when they came down to the hotel dining room for dinner, he asked her what she would like to have. The eyelashes fluttered and she bubbled, "I'd just adore a nice juicy steak!" He put down his cocktail, gave her a withering stare and said, "On Friday? What the devil kind of Catholic are you?" Evidently he was long on faith and short on morals.

If fish is not quite synonymous with Catholicity, for a time it was almost so with Christianity. I don't know who first wondered what would have happened if the Apostles had been butchers, but they were not; and yet it is remarkable how often fish glide between the lines of the New Testament. Our Lord performed no less than five miracles involving fish. The two occasions when He miraculously multiplied the loaves and fish seems to have canonized the fish in Christian tradition. The early Church saw in the multiplication of the loaves a foreshadowing of Christ multiplied in the Bread of the Eucharist. But the fish were part of that miracle, so the first Christians looked upon the fish too as a sacred symbol.

The day when Jesus healed Peter's mother-in-law, He worked a wonder that must have made Peter's mouth open wider than any fish that ever snapped at a shred of bait. Apparently Peter had just left the house when he was stopped by two officials who bluntly demanded the temple tax due from himself and Christ. (This is the ironic reverse of the collection we Catholics used to call "Peter's Pence," because here Peter is asked to do the contributing toward the upkeep of the temple.)

As soon as Peter returned, Jesus told him: "As to that tax, go down to the shore. Cast in your line. In the mouth of the first fish that leaps to it you will find a coin. Use it to pay my tax and yours." Peter had seen Christ with a gesture hush an angry, frothing sea into a stretch of smooth blue silk; but he must have been just as astonished when he opened that fish's mouth and found glinting there a silver coin, the precise amount for the double tax.

Scores of spiritual writers have conjectured about the natural cynicism that must have been Peter's initial reaction to still another "fish miracle." That one involved not a line but a net. It came down to this: What did a carpenter know about fishing? Peter and his group had been fishing all night and had caught nothing. Now the small craft came crawling wearily to shore through the pearly light of the dawn, the idle sail rustling like a drunk mumbling in his sleep. Jesus said: "Go back a little and cast the net to the right!" They did, and to Peter's amazement the net almost burst with its one hundred and fifty-three fish.

But the best was yet to come. There on the shore Jesus waited by the glowing fire He had built, with fish sizzling on the hot stones. Not only did He serve the Apostles, but (as Luke reminds us) He Himself partook of the meal He had prepared. And this was after Calvary! The hands that offered them the fish bore the scarlet scars of the nails. A phantom does not eat fish. So, in its own prosaic way, a fish becomes proof of the Resurrection.

Most of His adult life our Blessed Lord had spent plying the tools of the carpenter. As such, He had known the feel of the dryest of things: old wood, chips, sawdust. Later His hands must have come to know the soggiest feel — slimy scales and dripping tails. But He used the fisherman's catch to make one of His strongest points. When the catch is emptied out, He said, then comes the sorting. Now the worthwhile fish are carefully placed into baskets, while the useless are contemptuously tossed away. Thus shall it be, He warned, with the great net of the Last Judgment.

When you next look down upon your plate and see a fish, see a bit beyond it. A fish in its own quiet, historic way can be an unpretentious reminder of penance, of the Eucharist, of the Resurrection, and of the final separation of the saved and the lost.

chapter eight

FIRST LADY

{ The Beads }

As Saint Joseph is associated with the sawdust and shavings of a carpenter shop, and Saint John the Baptist with locusts and wild honey, and Saint Blaise with candles under the throat, Saint Dominic echoes to the rattling of the beads. We speak of a Jesuit college, a Benedictine abbey, a Redemptorist mission, a Paulist publication, and a Dominican rosary.

In our day there are those who frown down their liturgical noses on the beads. They shrug them off as a sort of spiritual security blanket, suited in its day for childish Catholics but now outmoded and outdated, a devotional dinosaur, a fossil fragment from a more fervent past.

Fortunately Vatican II sees the rosary through more rose-colored spectacles. While the Second Vatican Council does not use these precise words, it does imply that the Christian soul is irrigated by two spiritual streams: the liturgy and popular devotions. "Popular" means devotions accepted by the people. Not, of course, every new-fangled, "here today, gone tomorrow" religious novelty, but those devotions stamped with the sterling mark of the centuries. Certainly the rosary has rippled through the fingers of men who have drawn on gauntlets of steel to go off to the Crusades — as far back as that! About such time-tested devotions Vatican II has said that these are not only permitted but "warmly commended." Note again: not just allowed or tolerated . . . but warmly commended!

Is it any wonder then that every pope of this century (with just two exceptions) has written a special letter to the Catholic world endorsing the beads? The two exceptions are John Paul I who was in office only a month (some call him the patron of temporary employment) and therefore scarcely had time to send out a rosary encyclical. The other is the present John Paul II who has let his publicized actions speak for him by leading the rosary in several churches.

When the Mass in the vernacular began to ring out in our churches, the rosary went into temporary exile. There is, of course, no possible comparison between the Eucharist and the beads. In the old days at a Sunday Mass the priest performed the sacred ritual in a language the people could not understand, in a voice they could not hear, and with his face in the opposite direction. Bulky Sunday Missals then were few and far between. Missalettes were unheard of. So it was natural for a pious Catholic, attending Mass, to slip into a pew, fish out his beads, and quietly say the rosary. The priest at the altar did not bother him, and he did not bother the priest. The priest minded his business and the man in the pew minded his. They were both broadcasting to God but on different frequencies.

Now everything is different. The Mass is said aloud in the language of the people, and the people are supposed to participate. The harsh but just conclusion is that in ordinary circumstances the beads have no place in any hands during the holy sacrifice of the Mass. But, once you rule the rosary out-of-bounds during Mass, you have leveled the only prohibition against it. In all other circumstances the beads are perfectly in place: for example, at a wake.

There are Christian wake services that ignore the beads, and such a service is anyone's option. In some parts of the country many of the people at the wake would be Protestants and the rosary might just bewilder them. If, of course, the priest presiding explained each mystery briefly and pointed out that we are supposed to ponder that event, and that the Hail Marys are only a verbal tribute and a measure of time, those not of the Catholic faith might learn for the first time what a rosary is all about.

On the other hand, there are areas where the murmur of the beads around the casket is an almost sacred tradition. At any event, the choice should be laid before the mourners. How cruel it would be in an hour when mind and heart are in dark distress to force upon them an unwelcome ceremony!

What is difficult to understand, however, is the rejection of the rosary because it is not "scriptural." But the "Our Father" (six times in the rosary) is lifted right out of Scripture. The first half of the Hail Mary (the major part) is all scooped out of Scripture. And when we say the beads, we are supposed to meditate on the mysteries of the rosary. But all the joyful mysteries, all the sorrowful mysteries, and three out of the five glorious mysteries — those events in the life of our Lord or our Lady — are pages torn right out of Scripture.

I would like to repeat an anecdote that I described earlier in this book about John Cardinal Wright, who at his death was in charge of the clergy throughout the world. He said, "When I am laid out, please pray the rosary. And if nobody in the room has a pair of beads, look in my pocket. You will," he added with an impish grin, "find a pair there, unless the undertaker has taken them out." Cardinal Wright had a Cadillac brain, but he loved our Lady with the warmth and simplicity of an affectionate child.

Speaking of great minds, one thinks of that distinguished Jesuit Father Karl Rahner. He was possibly the most influential theologian of our times. On one occasion he had to deliver a lecture in the United States on some abstruse point of theology to a learned assembly of his colleagues. Conscious of his heavy Teutonic accent, he arranged with a young American priest to read his lecture for him. While the young, clear-voiced cleric read the profound treatise, Father Rahner sat at the side of the stage saying his beads. Probably more listeners were impressed and influenced by that than by the precisely argued theological treatise.

If Matt Talbot had been in the hall that night, the theological exposition might have gone over his head like the airmail. Matt Talbot, as you may recall from an earlier reference in this book, was the Dublin drunkard who bounced from the gutter to the stars. His cause for canonization has been introduced. As a laborer he had become an alcoholic, but by fierce prayer and grim courage he had won the battle of the bottle. He used both the liturgy and popular devotion. Every morning he stood outside the church, waiting for the doors to open for the first Mass. While he stood there, the beads went slowly through his workman's hands, tough and callused. And they were just as much at home there as in the frail fingers of an aged and saintly nun.

I still can remember, though it is fifty years ago, a blind lady in the Bronx to whom I brought Holy Communion each First Friday. She lived on the fourth floor of a tenement. Everything was poor but clean and neat. She had a pair of beads hanging like a tiny harness on the arm of almost every chair. She explained it was so easy to drop the beads or mislay them, and in this way she wasted no time. I feel sure she went to heaven on a beaded blanket of Hail Marys.

The blind are said to have a more delicate sense of touch than sighted persons, and this suggests another reason for the popularity of the rosary down the ages. The beads are a physical article, not a sacrament but a sacramental. The sacraments promote the proposition that we are not just spirits like the angels. We have a soul but also a body with its physical senses. The sacraments are material channels through which God sends invisible spiritual graces. In baptism He uses water; in Holy Communion, bread; in the sacrament of the sick, oil.

In a similar way the beads are a material thing, a physical article. They nestle in our hand, they rustle through our fingers. It is a distinctive outward sign. It is a tool in the hands of a workman of God.

It takes only ten minutes to say the beads in private. Hold on to them! They are Mary's apron strings, and if we grasp them we can never wander far from her!

{ Thoughts in the Temple }

On November 21 the Church keeps the anniversary of an event which is not set down in Scripture but which does have deep roots in ancient Christian tradition. The feast of the Presentation of Our Lady recalls that glorious day when, just as debutantes are presented to society, Mary was presented to God. Christian art has always loved to portray that scene, as Mary, a graceful child flanked by Saint Anne, her mother, and Saint Joachim, her father, ascends the broad steps of the temple, and is received at the top by the high priest in his ceremonial robes.

There for a few years, in the temple of Jerusalem, Mary studied the sacred scrolls. Did her finger tremble as it traced the verse which prophesied that a virgin would bring forth the Messiah? Hardly, for in her humility Mary never dreamed that this had anything to do with her. There, in the temple, Mary learned to weave the cloth of gold that hung before the great tabernacle containing the two stone tablets of the Ten Commandments. Little did she realize then that for nine precious months her body would be the tabernacle of the Lord of the Law, the Redeemer Himself.

There, in the temple, Mary learned to pray. How far from her thoughts, though, the incredible truth that one day the whole Christian world would be pleading for her prayers: "Holy Mary . . . pray for us sinners . . . now and at the hour. . . ." There, in the temple, she presented God with the most perfect gift He had ever received: a soul not only innocent of everyday sin but even of original sin, a soul as immaculate as the fresh-fallen snow on a cathedral spire, unsmudged by any grime of earth.

Perhaps you are thinking: This is all very well, but what does it mean here and now to us? Those quiet years that Mary spent with the other students in the annex of the temple, those years of cloistered dedication and sheltered training — all those years have little to do with us who live in today's hectic world and are pressured by all sorts of modern problems. Our Lady's life in the temple may well be a guide for novice nuns tiptoeing with downcast eyes along hushed convent corridors, but what message can it possibly have for people in the rat race of contemporary modern life?

In the first place I am not sure that convent corridors are so quiet nowadays; but I am sure that Mary in the temple — separated from the world — is a blunt reminder to us all that unless we also occasionally go apart in spirit, then sooner or later we shall spiritually come apart. To live with any measure of dignity and purpose, a man must dedicate his life to something. Mary dedicated her life to God. To what shall we dedicate our lives? Mere rhetoric would go on to ask: "Will it be the amassing of wealth? The pursuit of pleasure? The reaching out after power? The achievement of social status?" But gray experience knows that most people struggle desperately just to survive. Their chief dedication is to keeping the family's economic head above the constantly rising tide of debt.

Still, is there no more to life than bread on the table, clothes on the back, and a roof overhead? Give an animal food, shelter, and warmth, and it is content. In man's case, however, he was made to know, love, and serve God; but this we shall never do unless every now and then we retire into the crimson-curtained temple of our own heart, and there think about God and the things of God. How does He fit into the picture of my life? How much does He mean to me? Otherwise, God will soon become like a magazine whose subscription I have stopped, or a telephone I have had disconnected.

Too soon the dust of routine settles on our daily prayers. Too soon the cobwebs of custom hang upon our weekly communions. Too soon our souls become like musty attics cluttered with things that once were useful and valuable but now have lost their immediate meaning.

In televised football games there is a gimmick called "instant replay" by which a decisive play is promptly run off again, often in slow motion. The viewer then can notice things he never caught the first time. By the same token, perhaps we could profit by a second and more revealing look at some of the phases of our spiritual life. Take prayer, for one. Are we just going through the motions? We smile so patronizingly, for example, at the peasant of India who ties his pious petition to the spoke of a little prayer wheel, and then placidly rotates it, perfectly assured that each time this fluttering strip whips around, his prayer rises once more to heaven. But do we not say our morning prayers or our night prayers almost as mechanically? Is it not merely the automation by machine lips of a holy formula, while our minds and hearts are far away?

This, surely, is not the way Mary prayed in the temple.

She really prayed. Many of us just say prayers. Between praying and saying prayers flows a wide and deep ocean. In hospitals people really pray. In courtrooms they pray. On battlefields they pray. During storms at sea they pray. In classrooms at examination time they pray. They pray because their hearts and souls are in it. They are not just beating their lips in staid and stale phrases. In genuine prayer there glows an eager spark that easily leaps the gap between us and God.

Or suppose we saw an instant replay of our last few confessions. Would we not see ourselves plodding along in the rut of routine? God help us, we often go to confession so mechanically that the confessional seems only like a vending machine where absolutions are dispensed, or like a kind of spiritual turnstile through which we go clicking on our way to the communion rail!

Maybe we would help ourselves to a fresh and fervent approach to confession if we reminded ourselves that the confessional has nothing to do with confession. For what is a confessional? It is so much lumber and nails, so much curtain and screen, with perhaps a light that flashes on and flicks out. But all this has no more to do with sorrow for sin or pardon of sin than a judge's black robe and mahogany gavel have to do with justice. Probably the best confessions ever made were made miles away from any confessional: like a Marine kneeling in the mud alongside a chaplain sitting on an empty ammo box, or a passenger on the tilted deck of a disabled ship, or a patient in a hospital room on the eve of major surgery.

What makes a good confession is not the furniture around us but the dispositions inside us. If there is real sorrow for the past, and strong resolve for the future, it is a good confession. Going in or coming out of a confessional box has nothing to do with being sorry for one's sins.

Or, what if we saw an instant replay of our most recent Holy Communion? True, we are only human beings, and mysteries are not our meat, and the good God does not expect too much of us. But should we not occasionally prod ourselves into realizing what happens when we receive? The key word is realize. We know, all right. We do not need instruction. What we need is to be shaken out of our snug and smug cushion of taking it all for granted. We approach the altar without being the least bit awed. We are hardly even impressed.

Why does not that overwhelming truth sink into us, namely that when we walk back from communion we have within us for those few precious minutes, Almighty God Himself, the Creator; the God of the high, snowcapped mountains and of the deep, foam-crested seas; the God of the softly painted flowers and of the hard, blazing gems; the God of the child's clear eyes and the scholar's intricate brain; the God who became so small in the straw of Bethlehem and even smaller in the white Host? If we realized this, would we not be stirred to awe and reverence and gratitude and love?

In brief, like Mary in the temple, it pays to go apart at times from the noise of the world, and to think. Chesterton once said that the world would never grow dull for lack of wonders but for lack of wonder. So let us rouse ourselves to the spiritual wonders about us; but as we lay it on the line to ourselves we should remember this: When Cicero finished speaking, the crowd would say, "How well he speaks!" — and then go home. But when Demosthenes spoke, the crowd would cry out, "Let us march!" — and do something about it. If we make our thoughts in the temple have an impact on our daily acts, then our prayers will become more meaningful, our confessions more sorrowful, and our communions more fruitful. They will really affect our spiritual life!

{ Novena }

Time was when "novena" was an accepted term in any Catholic vocabulary. To define it would be like defining "holy water"; everybody knew it, so why explain? It was a "given." But alack and alas, times change. Now it is an exceptional parish that has a well-attended novena. So you *can* ask what the word does mean and what in the world ever happened to it.

Like most ecclesiastical terms or church words, *novena* in its origin bubbles up from the remote Latin, and means "nine in a row." If Julius Caesar had anticipated Abner Doubleday and invented baseball, dividing the diamond into three bases instead of Gaul into three parts, he would have called nine innings a novena, because novena in Latin means a series (though not a world series) of nine. In the Church too, novena implies a series of nine consecutive days of devotion. Sometimes this is stretched to stand for one particular day (like Tuesday or Wednesday) flowing through nine weeks. If this sort of sequence goes on all through the year, it is called a perpetual novena. For example, in our basilica every Wednesday is Novena Day.

To establish a basis for all this, do not turn to Holy Scripture. True, some "novenites" like to recall that when our Lord sent the Apostles back to pray on Ascension Thursday (for the coming of the Holy Spirit), it was after nine days of prayer that the Holy Spirit did descend upon the Apostles in the form of tongues of fire hovering over their heads, like the scarlet skullcaps of the bishops they were to become.

During the Middle Ages the people of Spain used to gather in their churches on the nine days before Christmas. This was a pious gesture toward the nine months of the Child Jesus in the womb. Perhaps "nine" should be con-

141

sidered just an indefinite sacred number like the forty days of the Old Testament! Just a convenient number on which to hang our prayers. We must never deify any number. We adore Christ; we venerate our Lady and the saints; but we do not worship the number nine or any other digit.

Having said this, let us also say that a novena can be a source of spiritual enrichment to anyone who participates. There are of course those who look down their liturgical noses and dismiss the novena as so much pious bric-a-brac, spiritual snow pudding, a sweet and frothy holy nothingness. In that case, let them go back to the documents of Vatican II and learn that the soul is nourished by cargoes carried on two roads: the liturgy *and* popular devotion.

Popular devotion is not to be scorned like the stepchild in the old novels. It has its rights. Novenas are not novelties. They go back a long way, and as such, according to the Second Vatican Council, are not merely permitted or reluctantly tolerated but "warmly recommended." I cite just one papal endorsement. Pope Paul VI was not on the throne of Peter three months when he sent a letter to the Redemptorist major superior granting a plenary indulgence to anyone who would make the nine Tuesdays or Wednesdays in honor of Our Mother of Perpetual Help. (The writer disclaims objectivity in this report because for the last forty-five years he has conducted this novena at the Basilica of Our Mother of Perpetual Help in Boston.)

One thing everyone has to admit: A devotion like this brings religion into the average layman's ordinary life. Sunday Mass is an obligation of law, but attendance at a weekday novena is an exercise of love. It means that with a warm gesture of spiritual generosity a Catholic cuts a sizable wedge out of the week and offers that time to our Lady, or to some particular saint. It is a wad of devotional yeast that brings the whole week to a higher level. We can never give God equal time, but the novena guarantees Him at least a smidgen more. Call it, if you will, something extra but not something superfluous. Don't we all have to be reminded of God and our Lady and the saints between Sundays? Here is an opportunity to recharge the spiritual batteries in a grimy weekday world.

Some Catholics sniffingly put down novenas as "the pious gimmes." To them the average novena-goer attends the novena somewhat like a parishioner at the wishing well of the church fair; only instead of a fishing pole the participant has a novena booklet of prayers. They come "to get their wish." They light vigil lights like punching numbers on a board, hoping their favor is under the right vigil light.

Some "novenites" may actually have this attitude. In any crowd there have to be some clinkers, whether it is a political rally or a union picnic. Why should the novena assembly hope to be different? There will be those who come, brooding, "No health, no house, no job, no boyfriend — novena!" These will pray for Uncle Arthur's arthritis, for young Tommy's tonsils, for Phil's success in physics, or for the right apartment in the right neighborhood at the right price.

But is this entirely wrong? Our Lord said, "Seek ye first the kingdom of heaven"; but that leaves some seconds and thirds, doesn't it? Did He not tell us to ask, "Give us this day our daily bread"? Communion would be nobler, but He did not rule out bread. When He stretched out His hand and drew Peter up from the sucking waves, He saved Peter's body, not his soul. When Christ touched blind eyes, He restored sight but did not grant salvation.

Go through the Gospels and you will find our Blessed Lord quietly acquiescing to prayers for material things and never forbidding the presentation of any urgent human need. The blind and the lame, the deaf and the mute — all had their prayers answered. If praying for something less than salvation is to be branded as "the gimmes," does not our Lady herself come under this blanket indictment at Cana? "They have no wine" was a mother's soft and subtle way of saying, "Son, won't you get this embarrassed couple out of their predicament?"

Novenas to some may seem like merely spiritual bon-bons: colorful and sweet but not very nutritious for a soul that needs sturdy nourishment. Yet I think, as in so many other areas, we take out of novenas what we bring to them. If our attitude is right and our motive high, a novena can be a perpetual open channel not only for material favors but also for bright flowering graces.

A half century ago I used to preach the Miraculous Medal Novena each Monday night, in a church on the Lower East Side of New York City. This particular evening I heard that one of the curates had taken ill during the past week and was in the neighboring hospital. On the way home I dropped in to visit him. He was far worse than I had been given to believe.

Father Formosa was Maltese and one of the most handsome men I ever saw. (His name — "Formosa" — meant handsome.) Against the pale pillow he looked like a dark Italian prince with flashing eyes and gleaming teeth. He looked up at me with a weak smile and said. "This is Monday, isn't it? And you have just come from the novena. Would you mind doing it all over again? I mean the prayers." His smile widened. "Not the sermon. That might finish me off. The novena booklet is on my table."

I picked up the booklet, dropped to my knees, and said the prayers more devoutly, I must confess, than I usually did. At the end he said, "Put the booklet under my pillow. I have a feeling I won't need it any more."

I said, "What do you mean? You're only thirty-five." Again the handsome smile and a slight shake of the head. The next morning I heard that he had died during the night. Somehow I have always felt that his little novena booklet was like a passport to Paradise, a letter to the Queen of Heaven introducing a saintly man who had served her not with the length of his years but by the depth of his love.

Novenas may not be for everybody, but they never hurt anybody. And they have helped many. Attend them or skip them, but don't knock them.

{ Umbrella or Lightning Rod? }

For some people a novena is only a spiritual umbrella. For others it is a lightning rod.

On a stormy day we are quite conscious of the many umbrellas in the church. But who ever thinks of the lightning rod high above the church? There is, of course, a Grand Canyon of difference between an umbrella and a lightning rod. For one thing, the umbrella is a much fancier item, at least as the ladies press a button and explode those domed rainbows. Men's umbrellas have no more color or style than different sections of a chalkboard. But a lady will insist on a whirl of gay circles or a picturesque plaid, and of course always there is the gleaming ornamental handle.

But consider, on the other hand, the lightning rod. It has no color, no pattern, no frills at all. The engineers mutter something about "Form follows function." And this is the story of the lightning rod. It is simple, plain — even grimly severe.

This too is the description of the average novena: simplicity itself! Even in the days when the Church employed ceremonial, ritualistic, majestic Latin, the novena was using ordinary, simple everyday English. When the Mass was a solo performance, the private preserve of the priest — who spoke something people could not hear, in a language they could not understand, and with his face turned in the opposite direction — the novena director was facing the people and using the language of the sidewalk and the subway. There were no frills, no processions, no important or imported preachers, no novelties whatever.

It was always the same simple program inside the same unvarying half hour. In fact the format was so simple that it is pleasant to recall that once during the Second World War a Catholic chaplain in the South Pacific merely tacked a picture of Our Mother of Perpetual Help to a coconut tree and there quietly conducted a routine novena service.

But let's get back to the umbrella and the lightning rod. Comes a slanting shower or a driving rain, and up pops the umbrella between us and the wet. In pretty much the same way, there are people for whom, whenever a slight shower of trouble begins pelting down upon them, up goes a novena like an umbrella between them and the trouble!

This, of course, is perfectly proper; but over and beyond that, should not our novena be up there all the time, the way a lightning rod is always over a church? The purpose of the lightning rod is not to keep us from getting wet, but to keep us from getting killed. It is *far* above us to preserve us during the major storms that crackle around every life, against temptations that may leap at us like a flash of blue lightning. It stands there against the black clouds of despondency that lower around us with stifling fear. Discouragement — not the devil — leads most people into grave sins. But a perpetual novena lifts our hearts and hopes on high. Like the lightning rod, it points always upward. It reminds us that though we may not get the favors we are asking here and now, we always get the courage to face whatever we must.

If you open an umbrella and shoulder your way

through a gusty, whipping rainstorm, the chances are that the umbrella may swish inside out. Its ribs are so frail and the storm so strong! That is a picture of some people and their novena. Perhaps they do not get what they are praying for, or perhaps they find themselves loaded with an unexpected cross, or perhaps they suffer reverses (and you know what a reverse means): their novena flips inside out. They give it up. Before this they were so pious and devout. Now they are sour and sullen and bitter.

With the lightning rod it is just the opposite. It is made for trouble! Certainly it smiles and gleams in the sunshine, but it also shines bravely in the rain. And it lifts its head proudly, almost like an aggressive chin pointed right at the storm. No matter what blow falls, the lightning rod will safely carry the shock down to the earth; and after the storm has roared itself tired, the lightning rod emerges again, serene in the sun.

As a rule, nobody is too attached to an umbrella. There is, to be sure, a light loop on milady's umbrella, but that is the only hold it has on us. That is why we can so easily lose our umbrella, or forget it, or mislay it, or leave it in the corner and ignore it. And some people act just that way with a novena. But the lightning rod is quite a different proposition. It is both bolted to the top of the church and sunk deep in the soil under it. The only way that the lightning rod normally becomes separated from the church is when they tear down the church. Otherwise it is a lifetime possession. And, in the same way, the only thing that separates a genuine lover of our Lady from his novena is the tragic fact of death. The novena is a lifetime possession too. Genuine lovers of our Lady will do anything except give up their devotion to her.

Some years ago, in an Eastern city, an alarm went out, an "All Points Bulletin" for a certain criminal. He was not a vicious criminal, not a violent man, not a robber nor a rapist nor a murderer. His field was forgery, and there he just kept forging ahead. But now the word filtered down to the police that he had returned to his native city. Detectives knew that he had been an avid baseball fan, so they watched the local ball field, the turnstiles, the grandstands, the bleachers. Not a trace. They knew that he had also followed the horses, so they kept a keen eye on the paddock, the grandstand, the betting windows. Not a sign.

Then came, from a stool pigeon, a curious fragment of information. Whenever this missing man had taken a couple of drinks he was likely to propose a toast to his mother. He boasted that she had been a living saint. In his mind there never had been another human being like her. One detective got the idea that since Memorial Day came that week, perhaps the missing man might visit her grave, so from behind a clump of bushes a pair of detectives watched the spot, from morning to night.

Memorial Day morning the cemetery gates were opened, and the people poured in. The sun went down, and the people poured out. The moon rose and turned the headstones to shafts of silver, but still no criminal. The two detectives on the last shift were about to call it all off. "Let's go home. He may have loved his mother once, but the spark has gone out. Let's go."

Just then, out of the shadows stalked a figure carrying a small wreath. He propped it against his mother's tombstone and knelt on the dewy grave. At that moment the pair of detectives advanced with drawn guns. The criminal did not seem surprised. In fact he seemed to expect something like this. He looked up at the revolvers and then down at the grave and murmured, "Mom, you were worth it. They knew nothing could keep me away from you."

We cannot kneel by the grave of our Mother Mary. For one thing the feast of her assumption reminds us that there never was a tomb or a relic of our Lady. Body and soul, she is in heaven. But her presence there is the very pledge of her power to help us here. Because she was a human being like ourselves, she pities us because of our problems. But because she is also the Mother of God, she has power to do something about them. Mary can intercede with her Son to reach out His omnipotent arm and lift us up when we have fallen, guide us back to the right path when we have strayed, beckon us with His finger when we grow discouraged.

All this Mary can ask and obtain, if we have constant devotion to this Mother of never-ending help. In other words, we must think of our devotion to Mary not as a casual, occasional umbrella, but as a steady, enduring lightning rod. Perpetual help demands perpetual devotion.

{ Death Comes to the Madonna }

In the Hail Mary we ask our Lady to pray for us at the hour of our death. *Our* death. But Mary died too, and the world's great museums display famous paintings as pious artists imagined that scene. Christian art always tends to be idealistic, so in the portrayal do not expect the raw untidiness of the real world. The chances are that the dying Mary of the art museum will by lying in an elegant canopied bed with the Apostles kneeling around her in their colorful cloaks like the richly tinted clouds of a grand sunset. This is not bad, because her going was like a sunset, the dimming and fading of a great light.

But do you suspect that such a scene is just pretty and picturesque piety? True, we do not know the physical circumstances of our Lady's passing. We do not know just where she died, or when, or how; that is, whether death resulted from some sickness or came simply as a result of old age. Yet we do know that because Mary was conceived without sin an atmosphere of quiet holiness always surrounded her, so that to the final feeble flutter of her heart Mary's soul was like a serene summer lake — unruffled by the slightest ripple of fear, of concern, of sadness.

Why is a man sad when the dark purple tide of death draws him away from this world? One reason is that he is leaving his loved ones. This sad parting is enough to draw any heart with sorrow and sprinkle it with tears. Still, in the case of our Lady, the two people dearest to her — Jesus, her Son, and Joseph, her husband — had already gone ahead, so that far from being crushed by a sense of parting, Mary was buoyed up by the thought of a happy reunion.

But besides tearful farewells, death can deal out other dark cards. And this causes some people to die not merely with reluctance or regret but with bitter resentment. Angry rebellion rumbles through their souls, because they must leave not only persons but things to which they were so deeply attached. Perhaps not till now did they realize that they had locked their hearts in their wallets or in their affluent lifestyle. And now death means waving a last and fast farewell to all the greenbacks in the bank and the blue-chip stocks — in a word, to everything.

Sometimes death comes to the modern pagan just when he thinks he has it made. He has arrived. He is a success. Now he stands in the spotlight of glory enjoying the attention, the admiration, the applause — even the envy of so many. But then without much warning the long skeleton arm of death reaches out and drags him down out of the spotlight into the darkness. The marble pedestal, on which he had just learned to stand so proudly, suddenly becomes his marble tombstone.

Samuel Johnson, perhaps the most prominent writer of his day, once visited David Garrick, certainly the most prominent actor, the toast of the British stage. The occasion was a housewarming for Garrick's new home. Johnson wandered through the luxurious mansion with its crystal chandeliers, its handsome furniture, its luxurious drapes, its wall bright with the paintings of great masters, and said simply, "David, it is going to be hard to leave all this behind."

Mary never had to face a separation like that. Her values were different. As with all saints, her treasures were not of this world. She had no straining cables to cut to get away. Her heart had long since been in heaven, and all she had to do now was to follow it. Her going must have been like a launched ship that slides easily down the ways and eagerly takes to the sea, the ocean of eternity.

Most of us are like our Lady at least in this, that we are not very rich. We do not live in velvet luxury; but there is in every one of us the natural tendency to treasure what we have, to cling to what we enjoy. That is why it is spiritually healthy to remind ourselves every now and then of that pointed admonition of Holy Scripture: "We have not here a lasting city, but seek one that is to come." And in that future place, "Eye hath not seen, nor ear heard what things God has prepared for those that love Him." Our physical existence ends at the grave, but our destiny soars far beyond.

Another factor that can frame death with terror is the memory of past sins. More than one dying man, propped up against his moist pillows, has found himself sitting in a reviewing stand, staring at the parade of past sins, each stopping to point an accusing finger ... so many unwelcome memories, ghosts of the shameful deeds of so many yesterdays.

Was the deathbed of Mary anything like this? How could it be? If memory did turn the pages of the book of her past, there were on the virgin pages no ugly blots of sin but only the golden record of constant virtue. Did she not practice patience in the poverty of Bethlehem, and purity amid the paganism of Egypt, and humility at Nazareth when the angel told her she was to be the Mother of the Redeemer? For her, dying meant only going to meet Him. When Mary was about to leave the world and looked back, she found no reason for remorse but only for relief. A responsible job well done, and now there was nothing left but to rejoin her Son.

On any sincere Christian deathbed too, there should be only strong confidence and deep trust in God's mercy. If we believe in Christ as our Savior, and rely on His promises, then no matter how low a man has sunk in the swamp of sin, as long as he crawls back to the cross, and looks up to those blood-rimmed eyes, and pleads for pardon, he will never die unforgiven. Why did Christ choose death by crucifixion except that the cross would be a symbol of arms outstretched in perpetual welcome to any sinner, to every sinner who comes stumbling back?

The trouble is we do not know if we shall have the chance to come back, if we delay. Voltaire, the philosopher who spent his life ridiculing and reviling religion, died screaming for a priest. His friends, so-called, would not let one near him. Louis XV, king of France, brazened it out to the end and then begged for the last rites (as the sacrament of the anointing of the sick used to be called). Henry VIII saw the plague striking victims all around him, so he sent away his mistress, Anne Boleyn, and slipped into a confessional. To someone like this who finds himself standing on the threshold of death, the two-pronged question "What is on the other side, and where am I headed?" can become a big black question mark that hooks him by the legs and drags him to his knees.

With Mary, there was no such question. She knew and she was happy to go home. Who can doubt that in heaven she was received by flights of bright angels and radiant archangels and escorted to the very throne of the Redeemer, her divine Son?

"Pray for us now and at the hour of our death." In that last hour when our glazed eyes turn toward her, may Mary reach down to take our trembling hands and lead us safely into eternity, with no regret at what we leave, no fear as to where we go, no despair at what we have done, but only feeling in our inmost soul quiet joy, the reward of having honored Mary as our Mother, and now as her faithful children, or even as prodigal sons and daughters, at last come safely home!

{ Above All Women Glorified }

Whether you look at the world through the vivid flashbacks of history (from diplomatic treacheries to slaughter-red wars) or down the headlight-lit avenue of the present (accounts embezzled, perjuries pronounced, bank vaults plundered), the world morally is a messy place. It all goes back, of course, to Adam and Eve and original sin; but since up to now the world has been dominated by men, most of the blame must be laid on their broad shoulders.

How much men have been influenced by their women we can only surmise. But it is no surmise that many of the important women of ages past have been somewhat south of sainthood. Queens in their rustling silks have strutted across the stage of history, stood for their brief moment in the bright spotlight, then slipped away into the wings — often being sent off, not with applause but with hisses!

If I mention ancient Egypt, do you not think of Cleopatra? Cleopatra, the seductive siren, the promiscuous wrecker of high-society homes! If I mention old Russia, there comes to mind Catherine the Great. The Great? More appropriate would be Catherine the cunning, the cruel, the dissolute. And France had its Madame de Pompadour, Madame du Barry, Catherine and Marie de Médicis. England had its Elizabeth I, known to some as Good Queen Bess, but not to that bright and blessed band of men whose corpses hung and swung from the grim gallows of Tyburn Tree, and who were barbarically disemboweled even while still alive.

Not too many queens of the past had a halo circling their crowns. Fame and prominence they may have had, but not piety or purity. At any rate, leave off poring over the yellowed parchments of the past and snap open your crackling morning papers. Does not the same type of woman come crashing through the columns, the famous and the stained, the well-known and the soiled? Not a queen perhaps, unless a queen of the screen or of the stage or of television, a prominent star, but so often a falling star!

You read that she has now entered her third marriage or is announcing her second divorce or has just decided to live with such and such a man. Some of these characters go through these casual alliances as often and as fast as a train through a tunnel, and like the train they come out dirtier every time.

When I was a boy I remember my mother singing an old favorite that had the words "Through the fields of clover we will ride to Dover on our golden wedding day." Stay married for forty-nine years and you are an obscure nobody. Survive one year more and you may make the inside pages of your local journal. On the other hand, you can be married only a year, and if you are notorious enough and the divorce trial is lurid enough, you will rate national coverage on page one.

News is usually either sinful or sad. Just being good never made the history books or the morning papers. To be quietly decent: a loving, devoted mother; a faithful hardworking father; an ordinary average family in an everyday run-of-the-mill home — what reporter ever whipped out his ballpoint pen to chronicle these? The media are not interested in the family circle. They drool, though, for the triangle: husband and wife and the other woman. Curiously, though, that third angle of the triangle, contrary to all the laws of geometry, is never angular. She is curvaceous and streamlined.

The point is that if decency is consistently overlooked and underplayed, while the scandalous is regularly showcased and glamorized, will not decency soon lose its influence and its impact? If goodness is ignored and the sordid and the seamy headlined and illustrated, is there not some danger that we may take it for granted that sin is in the saddle, that this is the way of the world, that "everybody does it"? Is there no present danger here that we may shrug our moral shoulders and fall in behind the insistent thump of the world's drum that booms, "Sin, sin, sin"?

This is precisely the time when we should tilt our ears to another sound, not of a padded mallet falling on a drumhead but of a heavy hammer clanking on iron spikes. And hear the groans of the Figure writhing on the cross! And recall the grim implications of Saint Paul, that while Christ was crucified once on Calvary, every serious sin is in its own diabolical way a recrucifixion.

Let the world and worldings call sin, especially sexual sin, by their own deceptive names (like romantic interlude or matrimonial misadventure or social indiscretion) — these are only like gilding the nails in a new crucifixion.

It will help the sincere to remember that under the first blood-running cross of Calvary there stood a woman, ashen-faced in her grief. Her name never streamed across any headlines, but that name, Mary (along with the memory of her example), reaches its long arm down even to our day. Mary's influence, when she left the world like a setting sun, fanned out in golden rays to embrace even the ends of the earth. Before her, history's queens are like bits of glass before a diamond. In her were miraculously merged virginal purity and divine motherhood.

Is it not comforting to realize that when it came to choosing a mother, God did not select some imperious beauty like Helen of Troy, whose face launched a thousand ships — nor the toast of the Middle Ages, Eleanor of Aquitaine, her of the golden hair and the violet eyes and the commanding presence? Instead the Almighty chose an obscure maid in an unknown village. To the world she was a nobody, but to the clear eye of heaven she was the fairest flower in the garden of the world. In her womb — like a pearl in a velvet case — the very Son of God would repose.

Was this not the highest compliment that humanity ever received, that God chose for His Mother not a fiery seraph but a human being like ourselves? He chose a woman whose goodness, while she lived, was never "news," never blared about, never headlined. But through the centuries her quiet greatness began to be recognized, and in her honor cathedrals lifted their lofty, majestic spires; artists painted their glowing Madonnas; musicians sent spiraling up their silvery Ave Marias.

To her throne today armies of Hail Marys march. From her fingertips favors and graces pour down like waterfalls. Mary of Nazareth, so unknown, became Mary of everywhere. From anywhere a prayer can reach her, and an answer will come smiling down!

chapter nine

BASKET OF FRAGMENTS

{ **Crucifix in the Classroom** }

Since excellent public schools are available in most areas, the question arises, high as a church steeple and pointed as its spire, "Why burden the good people with a parochial school?" Some might hold that such a project is not only uneconomical but also unecumenical, and therefore divisive and un-American. But here it might be well to remind ourselves that in the Constitution there is no mention of public schools; that not one of the fifty-six signers of the Declaration of Independence ever attended a public school; that we were fifty years a nation before we ever had a public school, and almost a hundred years in existence before we had a president who had seen the inside of a public school. The original, traditional school of this country was a private religious school, and it is precisely this attitude of early America — namely that religion is a vital part of education — that makes Catholics build parochial schools today.

When the Founding Fathers championed "freedom of religion," they never thought it would end up being "freedom *from* religion." They wanted the equality of all religions — not the absence of every religion. To them a classroom without prayer would have seemed a strange classroom indeed. Is a Catholic school less patriotic because it also teaches the things of God? Why did J. Edgar

Hoover, then head of the Federal Bureau of Investigation, and not a Catholic, say publicly that the Catholic school system was the greatest grant ever given to the United States, greater in its benefits to the country than the Rockefeller Fund or the Carnegie Foundation?

Possibly Hoover may have been thinking that you find no Communists coming out of Catholic schools, but the well is deeper than that. It goes down to the basic principle that every man should be convinced that the religion he follows is the true religion; otherwise why follow it?

Ecumenism should mean that you pray for your brother to come into the true religion and that you give good example that he may do so. You respect and honor him for following his conscience, but that does not make you dilute what you hold as true, or whittle down one sliver of it in order to win him over. You go on speaking what you believe are the words of truth in the tones of love.

By the same token you want your children taught the truth, the true faith — and you do not believe it can be done well unless it can be done on a regular schedule. Faith should be an essential part of a parochial school curriculum or the school is a failure. To the library a man may be a card, to the post office an address, to the registry of motor vehicles a license, to the army a serial number; but to the Catholic school the scholar is a soul.

We sometimes say that a man is a good hand at carpentry, or that he has a good head for figures, or that he has a good ear for music. But the Catholic school holds that man is not just head or hand or ear or even heart, but above all, soul — that is, a spirit within him that will never die, a spirit that was made "to know God, to love Him, to serve Him, and to be happy with Him in eternity."

Certainly the mind must be trained. Certainly the standard of education in parochial schools must conform to the demands of the state; otherwise, the state could rightly close the parochial schools, and parents would avoid them. But, at least in New England, where I have lived for more than forty years, the constant complaint till recently has been that you cannot get a seat in a Catholic school. Perhaps parents choose a Catholic school because of its stricter discipline; but this is part of the general religious atmosphere: obedience to lawful authority.

The parents who send a child to a Catholic school do so with the conviction that they are helping that child toward a happy eternity. Why else are we here on the earth? The narrow runway down which a plane roars before it soars into the sky seems a far stretch indeed as you view its long gray lane; but how insignificant it is, compared to the endless blue of the flight! This life is a runway whose only purpose is to help us soar to a happy heaven and not plummet to eternal destruction.

To achieve this, the Catholic parent feels that neither Sunday Mass nor Sunday school is enough; the training has to be deeper and even daily. Years ago I read of a young fellow who was sentenced to death in the electric chair for murder, and in that particular section of the country the formula of the judge concluded, "And may God have mercy on your soul!" (Just as we still have "In God we trust" on our coins.) The youth almost snarled, "Soul? You want to know something? I went through grammar school, high school, and the state college. This is the first time I was ever told I had a soul."

The time to begin to learn of the soul's eternal destiny is not in the electric chair but almost in the high chair. Education is not just for filling the head but fulfilling the heart and soul. It consists not in "information" but "in formation," the formation of character. Is it too strong to say that imparting information without inculcating morality is like loading books on an animal's back?

I remember doing research long ago at the Library of

Congress in Washington. All around were silent people busy at desks: pages turning, pens scratching, magnifying glasses focused — each student alone and absorbed. It was like a convention of lighthouses. One day two men stopped at one of the desks and took the occupant away. It turned out he was one of the most wanted counterfeiters in the country. He was as busy as anyone else — studying steel engravings in the library at the government's expense. This man obviously had intelligence, he had industry, he was acquiring information — but he did not have integrity.

Education alone does not produce goodness. Education is like a revolver; its use depends on whether it is in the hands of a gangster or a state trooper. The same skill that makes one man a topflight accountant can make the man in the next office a clever embezzler. To knowledge we have to join morality; and Catholics are convinced that the anchor of morality will drag unless it is hooked deeply into the riverbed of religion and God.

This then is the only reason for a Catholic school: that the child who enters it be trained not merely in mind but in soul; that he be prepared not only for this life but for the only reason God put us in this life, to merit happiness in the life to come.

Every Catholic school is a magnificent symbol of the vivid faith of the fathers and mothers and all other parishioners. It means they believe so deeply that they are willing to sacrifice generously.

Who can sufficiently praise the nuns that staff a Catholic school? They are giving more than money. They are giving themselves, everything. And the lay teachers — does anybody doubt they have to accept less in financial reward for this work? When you work for the Church you have to be dedicated. Financially, it is ridiculous; but spiritually, it is sublime.

Each Catholic school is an act of faith in tomorrow.

Though the building itself may one day crumble — like all other things human — the good that it does will roll on like waves to the very shores of eternity. And, as long as it stands, it will stand as a monument to zealous parishioners, for whom the faith comes first!

{ Fairy Tales on Celluloid }

Flicking through the pages of the morning prayer not too long ago and noticing a gossip column with the names of "talked abouts" in heavy black, I realized that my curiosity about the personal quirks of movie actors and actresses would not fill an underdeveloped thimble. Perhaps this is because I have been fortunate in never having read a fan magazine, and have no intention of filling this lamentable lack so long as the good Lord wills it. It may amaze some teenage girls, but it is a melancholy fact that I do not have the slightest interest in knowing why some male movie star prefers lavender socks or why some female idol is apt to turn pale at the mere buzz of a bumblebee.

Now an actor like Eddie Polo — he was something else. How many nights, I wonder, did I toss in my Brooklyn boyhood bed in scary nightmares that took us both through wild searches for the missing half of *The Broken Coin*, or on a panting flight from the curse of *The Violet Diamond?* It was long before radio, and I was all of ten years old.

All this came back to me one summer when I had a couple of weeks' vacation and a few nights of insomnia and the temporary custody of a television set. It was my first real encounter with the late show; and those fascinating reruns of films from long ago brought me back to the days when I was stationed in a parish in the Bronx and used to go to Radio City with a grizzled old fire chief who had a VIP pass.

The Depression of the 1930s was then at its somber height, and yet people kept going to the movies. They made sacrifices in other areas but managed to scrape up enough money for that one weekly recreation. To them the movies were a means of forgetting reality and of living for a little while in another world.

It was a kind of "tire-escape," that is, when you were tired of washboards and ironing boards, of switchboards and chalkboards (or blackboards, as they used to be called); when you were fed up with pushing a WPA wheelbarrow or pulling a WPA rake — when you were tired of all that, that little blue or pink movie ticket was your magic carpet that suddenly lifted you up and floated you away from the grimy world all around you to the glorious, gorgeous never-never land of make-believe.

A few moments after you brushed past the box office you were dancing in a resplendent uniform or in a shimmering gown under great crystal chandeliers to the enchanting music of "The Great Waltz." Or you were skiing down a Swiss Alp in a flurry of flying snow while the Matterhorn peaked in the background. Or you were idly tinkling the highball ice cubes on the afterdeck of a handsome yacht, gliding over a silver sea under a moon that must have come straight from one of Tiffany's more expensive shelves.

Anyway, when it was regretfully over, and you came stumbling out of the dark seats, blinking at the avenue's bright lights and gulping down the cool fresh air, you thanked heaven — and Hollywood — for a few merciful furlough hours spent away from the drab and dull world of reality in the wonderful and exhilarating and impossible land of make-believe. The movies were the adult's bedtime story, the grown-up's fairy tale.

Looking back now, it seems that the pictures came in different categories. They covered a few definite areas of life, and it was fun to recognize the props, human and otherwise. Nowadays a television set — where even basketball players are only eighteen inches tall — does not give the same sense of illusion; but when you were at a movie, you were there, right in the middle of it all.

If it was a newspaper picture, every city room was the same. You could count on half the men wearing green eyeshades and chewing black cigars, and the other half typing with tilted-back fedoras and puffing nervous cigarettes. The "cub" reporter always got his story and earned the grumbling commendation of the hard-boiled editor, who always was so crusty you suspected he sweated vinegar. But you knew too that he never would print the stuff that his more sophisticated successors think nothing of spraying across the current pages of what used to be considered a family newspaper.

Then there were the medical movies, and to see them again on TV makes you wonder if they make the present men in white see red. To the nostalgic viewer they are, despite their earnest drama, highly hilarious. But speaking of men in white, in those old hospital pictures everything is white: white operating-room masks (of course over the mask always a pair of dark eyes, questioning, challenging, defying), white gowns, white beds, white walls, white doors; in fact so many white doors opening and closing that you almost go snow-blind. When a commercial comes on and you go to the refrigerator, you would not be surprised if a white-uniformed nurse came out with a Coke. When you return, the surgeon's reflector is swinging ominously around like a beacon at an airport. Later, in the patient's room as the crisis builds, you see a close-up of the thermometer: 102, 103, 104 — it is like the elevator going up in a skyscraper. When it hits 105, there is a rolling crash of drums and the heroine-nurse clicks around the corridor corner wheeling an oxygen tank. And none too soon. The

Marines have made it again, but just. Anyway it's grand fun.

Cowboy pictures in the old days (the horse opera was long before the soap) had traditions of their own. Today's Marlboro Man, for all his make-up, looks as if he belonged to a real ranch; but the best of the old-time cowboys were really movie cowboys who dressed for the back-lot sets and the ogle of the Hollywood lens. Glittering spurs, lacquered boots, flapping polar-bear chaps, a handsomely brocaded vest, a dashing leather jacket fringed with golden strings like a parlor lamp, and, to top it all, a tall white Stetson soaring up like a New England steeple. If the average cow ever encountered a cowboy like this, America would face spates of curdled milk. When such a bespangled but leather-faced Westerner headed for the corral, he waddled like a pair of rhythmic parentheses. But when he vaulted into the saddle and rode off to Rattlesnake Gulch (reel three) or into the sunset (reel six) he took every city slicker's heart with him.

A faint demurral, though, because as he dashed off pronto on the pinto, he often rode roughshod over — well, perhaps not justice but certainly over — due process of law. Granted that Cactus-Beard Cagney had pumped a lot of lead into Shoulder-Shootin' Shorty, did that give Shorty's brooding brother the right to take the law into his own hands (it had been hanging conveniently on his hip) and drill that mangy Cagney critter with a vindictive thirty-eight? Do two wrongs add up to one right? Only in the weird arithmetic of Hollywood. Let it then be duly noted that morality — in the wider and true sense of the term — can be trampled under the thundering hooves of the Get-Even Kid just as surely as it can under the silver slippers of some sultry siren. Wild West can be as errant as Mae West.

Then there were the historical yarns, revived, or at least exhumed every now and then as technicolor pages from the picturesque past. Here the difficulty came in the clash between fact and fiction. The director cavalierly winks at "history" while he photographs "his story." I remember reading, eons ago, that Donald Ogden Stewart (a name in his day) complained that after spending three years researching and writing *Marie Antoinette*, the final version retained just one line from his script. I can believe that, because Bill Cunningham, a well-known Boston columnist and radio personality, said that he sent in a script about his early days in rural Texas. They kept one word, the title *Texas*, but paid him handsomely, so he literally put his pride in his pocket (or in his wallet, in this case).

In other words, the movies I was looking at during those late shows on television did not even pretend to mirror truth. They offered escape and entertainment. How else explain a slim heroine with a Parisian hairdo airing bedclothes on a tenement fire escape? Should there come a pelting deluge, said heroine would reappear with the coiffure discreetly moistened (or oiled) and every strand artistically anchored. She would look better groomed coming out of a tornado than most ladies coming out of a beauty parlor.

But in those simple days we loved it, and overlooked it, or perhaps never even noticed it. One scene stands out in a recent rerun, where boy and girl are at a lunch counter, and as he poises his cruller he looks into her eyes with a look far sweeter than the powdered sugar on the cruller, and murmurs, "We don't have much, dear, but we do have love." And as she gives him a smile like the aurora borealis, suddenly out of somewhere bursts the swelling crescendo of a fifty-piece orchestra, and you wonder: How did a symphony ever get into a beanery?

In all this "unreel" movie world, perhaps nothing was so far from grim fact as the presentation of death. Death that waits for no man, always humbly marked time for the man with the megaphone and the leather puttees and the canvas chair stenciled DIRECTOR. On the silver screen they die with such perfect diction, the right profile (get my good side), and the proper pauses. You could not but suspect that having wrung the last dramatic drop from the scene, the victim then would rise with regret, and reluctantly yield the camera to someone else. Such as these should be buried only in Forest Lawn.

Comes here, however, the disquieting thought that we should remember that when you are speaking of carefully contrived dying, even Shakespeare had his characters pass away in resonant iambic pentameters. There was Mercutio, for instance, gazing at the slash where Tybalt's sword had ripped through his chest. Someone asked in effect, "Are you badly hurt?" And he murmurs, "No, 'tis not so deep as a well, nor so wide as a church door, but 'tis enough, 'twill serve. . . ." What colorful imagery on the threshold of extinction! And then comes the deflating realization that Mercutio never gasped this while he was bubbling blood. A fellow named Shakespeare wrote it while he was quaffing port.

Similarly, in the general area of violence the movies can airily appeal to Master Will. Is anything more violent than Hamlet? Tick off the fatalities: two kings die, the queen dies, Polonius dies, Ophelia dies, Hamlet dies, Laertes dies. I think it adds up to one drowning, two poisonings, and four stabbings. The curtain falls on a scene that would make the Mafia look moderate.

One thing that stands out in film oldies is how Hollywood tilts the board in its own pagan favor. The good guy is so often a stiff, wooden character, a holier-than-thou creature, carrying around his virtue like a picket with a placard saying "I am good!" — and naturally you hate him. The naughty girl, on the contrary, is always a nice girl, gracious, vivacious, curvaceous, charming, disarming, completely attractive. To the hesitant hero she just flutters that forest of eyelashes and cutely pouts, "But what does your heart say?" Not what does your conscience say, or morality, or the Ten Commandments, or God, or even common decency — but "What does your heart say?" By the same token, suppose you see a long, shiny Cadillac drawn up at the curb. What does your heart say? Would you like it or not? But has a man any more right to run off with another man's wife than with his car? Civilization became civilization not by following the impulses of the jungle but by subduing them.

As pointed out earlier, it is curious that in Hollywood's version of the triangle (two men and a woman) the third angle is never angular. She is streamlined and shapely and lovely and lonely. As the other man confides to her that his wife does not understand him, slow tears (like pearls from a broken department-store necklace) skid down her cheek, or at least down the half-inch of make-up embossing it. You wonder how many a movie patron — because she is sitting there relaxed in the dark, and because she has previously checked her brains at the box office, and because she is being drowned in the sweet warm gruel of sentimentality — finds herself thinking, "Yes, they were meant for each other," forgetting that what God hath joined, not even Hollywood can put asunder.

Does this seem exaggerated? Will you take my word that I actually heard a wife in back of me at a movie a long time ago hiss into her husband's ear, "You see, Cary Grant dries the dishes!" It does have an impact.

Many of us never go to the movies. I have let a span of three or four years pass without looking at a big screen or listening to the rustle of candy wrappers. But almost all of us have television sets. From that gleaming box can come the same amoral outlook, the same pagan principles, the same un-Christian, distorted view of life.

The trick is to neutralize the intake with a spiritual counteragent like solid Catholic doctrine and a strong dash of common sense. So, if they show you suicide against a background of soft music to make it appear honorable and even brave; if they show you revenge against a background of majestic mountains and handsome horses and an orchestra of crackling pistol shots; if they show you adultery or divorce against a background of magnificent mansions and sparkling diamonds; if they show you evil dominating the fight for fourteen rounds and then in the fifteenth, virtue triumphs for the final two minutes, just say to yourself, "Well, it's been a nice *celluloid fairy tale*. Now, like Garbo, I tank I go home."

{ Ellen Parishioner, R.I.P. }

We knew her for so long, loved her so dearly, and now all we can do is whisper a fond farewell to the coffin in the middle aisle. In fact the trembling flame of the paschal candle seems like a tiny golden hand waving "Good-bye." Or is it rather what the Germans call *"Auf Wiedersehen"* or the French, *"Au Revoir"* — "Till we meet again"? Existence is not merely a matter of life and death, but of life and death and more life after that. Death is only the end of the beginning.

Ellen believed that and lived it. Even at the end, when she knew the spool of life was winding down with only a few frail inches left, she looked at the end with level eyes. In that last illness she used to say with a wan smile that weeping willows bear no fruit, and she was determined not to be a human weeping willow. God had given her a cross and Ellen early decided that it was easier to carry it than to drag it. God knew best. His holy will be done!

So her death was a carbon copy of her life. She had

spent her years following Christ, and now at death she had finally caught up with Him. So, if she heard His call so willingly, why should we resent her going? Never say about Ellen, "Too bad she died." Rather, "Thank God she lived!" Ellen's picture was never on the cover of *Time*, but her name is written in the Book of Eternity. Now she is happy that she tried to lead a *good* life and not just a successful one, "For all we can hold in our cold dead hands is what we have given away!"

In the memory of many, her example — please God — will go on. Robert Louis Stevenson wrote about an old Scottish gardener who was at last buried amid the roses he had nurtured all through the years. And Stevenson perceptively added, "Those roses still take their life from him, but in a new and more intimate way." So, out of her simple good life, even long after Ellen has gone, will bloom acts of kindness inspired by her memory.

In this swirling age of changes in the Church, she was a lingering, old-style Catholic — the kind of Catholic who built the parish church, paid for the parochial school, would not dream of missing a mission, subscribed to the-Lord-knows-how-many foreign mission magazines, loved her beads, attended the novena, and put God first in her life. Ellen pegged her calendar on dates like the First Fridays and the Forty Hours and the May procession and All Souls. In all this, it would never have occurred to her that her quiet goodness was like a church steeple that (just by being there) silently reminded other people of God.

They say of one of the Saint Gregorys, that when he went to a strange city to study, he got to know only two streets: the one leading to the school and the other to the church. In that respect, there were only two highways in Ellen's life: her family and her faith. As a devoted wife, dedicated mother, and grandmother, she lived for her loved ones. Her heart was in her family, and her family was in her heart. At the same time, as a staunch Catholic, Ellen poured herself into her religion. Her life ran like one straight avenue between her family table and the communion rail.

People like her make up the Church because basically the Church is not flowing vestments nor curling incense nor booming bells nor blazing windows. The Church is people, people just like Ellen, and each of us is diminished by her going. She was not unwilling to go, because toward the end she was weak and weary. Like a little child who puts her hand in her mother's, she whispered, "I'm tired. Please take me home." And our Lady, to whom she was so devoted, did just that.

We do not feel ashamed if, remembering this fine woman, we find quiet tears coming to our eyes. Melodramatic grief is out of place, but genuine sorrow is a natural and even a Christian reaction. It is only the iron-browed pagan, the cold modern pagan of a computer civilization, who scorns honest grief as watery weakness. Did not our Lord Himself feel tears come to His eyes at the tomb of His friend Lazarus?

At the funeral Mass for Ellen, the celebrant lifted the chalice of wine as an offering to God, but first into it there trickled a few drops of water. So into the wine of life's glowing joys some teardrops must fall. Our farewell to Ellen, like the sacrifice of the Mass, was a sacrifice of its own, as we offered up the loss of a loved one. In our sad, solemn hour, we stood beneath the cross with its shadow falling dark across our faces, and gave back to God someone that He in His goodness long ago gave to us.

Perhaps our first impulse is to begrudge her to heaven and wonder why God should take her even now. But then wisdom whispers that we see things only from the gopher hole of this earthly existence, whereas God looks down with a clear, long view from the mountains of eternity.

And, because He sees better, He knows what is best. Besides, is it ever too early for heaven? The hand of our Lord that strikes us at death is bored through with the red hole of a crucifixion nail. Our Lord died for us. Such a hand could never strike in malice but strikes only as the lifeguard strikes the struggling swimmer: for a greater good.

In the cross is our redemption. Look at the cross of Calvary from above, as from a helicopter, and it seems like a giant sword plunged into the hilltop, because by His dying our Redeemer slew eternal death. Look at the cross from below, and it looks like a huge key with the crossbar and notches pointing up as if to open heaven. If the loaded cross, sagging with Christ's Body, proved His love, the empty tomb and the glorified Body proved His power.

That Resurrection was more than a proof of our Savior's divinity. It was also a promise and pledge of our own personal resurrection on the last day. Our Lord's Resurrection established forever that death was not an end but a beginning. Death was not the blunt stop of a dead-end street. It was the start of a new, broader avenue. Death was not a wall. It was a door. Death is not the last line of the last page of the last chapter, sadly saying "The End." It is a brave flourish that writes "To Be Continued." In that sense we attended a graduation, a commencement, because Ellen had just been graduated from earth and had commenced a happy eternity.

For what had lain in Ellen's casket? Not the person we loved but only the shell that had been shed. There in that casket had rested only the broken cage. The bird — the spirit — had streaked off. There had reposed only the slowly crumbling body, the torn envelope. The letter, the message, the soul, was in the hands of God.

Since Ellen is with God and no longer with us, we shall miss her. It is as when a great tree falls and "leaves a lonely place against the sky." For when the tree falls, many feel the loss. The farmer loses his fruit, the birds their nests, the wayfarer his shade, the artist his subject. In the same way, many will feel the loss of Ellen — her family, her relatives, her friends, this parish, our neighborhood.

To her family especially we reach out the understanding hand of Christian sympathy. In that hand there is only stretched out the promise of prayers, because if Ellen could speak now, she would ask for prayers, not praise. To us she was a good woman, but every human has faults. Otherwise, that person would not be human, would in fact be a walking heresy, a living rebuttal to the doctrine of original sin.

What *we* think good may not be good enough for heaven. Standards are different. The surgeon who at breakfast dips his spoon into his cereal has clean hands, but he scrubs them far cleaner before he takes up the scalpel. How high are the standards of heaven? We do not know; but we should send our prayers after every departed soul, and if they be not needed for atonement and purification they will add to that soul's radiant glory.

As Ellen goes away from us, across the shadowy bridge of death toward the eternal shore, our eyes follow her sadly, but we should not stop here. This would be stopping at the bridge of death and thinking only of our loss. Cross the bridge, and think of her gain — and our heart leaps with the joy to realize that she has gone on to the bright company of the blessed. There, after life's weariness, comes welcome rest; after its suffering, blissful ease; after its turmoil, serene peace; and after a temporary separation, an eternal reunion.

May the Mother of Perpetual Help, to whom Ellen was so warmly devoted, intercede that the Perpetual Light shine upon her!

May she rest in peace. Amen.

172